AI
Driverless Cars
Realities

Practical Advances in
Artificial Intelligence and Machine Learning

Dr. Lance B. Eliot, MBA, PhD

Disclaimer: This book is presented solely for educational and entertainment purposes. The author and publisher are not offering it as legal, accounting, or other professional services advice. The author and publisher make no representations or warranties of any kind and assume no liabilities of any kind with respect to the accuracy or completeness of the contents and specifically disclaim any implied warranties of merchantability or fitness of use for a particular purpose. Neither the author nor the publisher shall be held liable or responsible to any person or entity with respect to any loss or incidental or consequential damages caused, or alleged to have been caused, directly or indirectly, by the information or programs contained herein. Every company is different and the advice and strategies contained herein may not be suitable for your situation.

ISBN: 978-1-73-460162-6

DEDICATION

To my incredible daughter, Lauren, and my incredible son, Michael.

Forest fortuna adiuvat (from the Latin; good fortune favors the brave).

CONTENTS

Dr. Lance B. Eliot

ACKNOWLEDGMENTS

I have been the beneficiary of advice and counsel by many friends, colleagues, family, investors, and many others. I want to thank everyone that has aided me throughout my career. I write from the heart and the head, having experienced first-hand what it means to have others around you that support you during the good times and the tough times.

To Warren Bennis, one of my doctoral advisors and ultimately a colleague, I offer my deepest thanks and appreciation, especially for his calm and insightful wisdom and support.

To Mark Stevens and his generous efforts toward funding and supporting the USC Stevens Center for Innovation.

To Lloyd Greif and the USC Lloyd Greif Center for Entrepreneurial Studies for their ongoing encouragement of founders and entrepreneurs.

To Peter Drucker, William Wang, Aaron Levie, Peter Kim, Jon Kraft, Cindy Crawford, Jenny Ming, Steve Milligan, Chis Underwood, Frank Gehry, Buzz Aldrin, Steve Forbes, Bill Thompson, Dave Dillon, Alan Fuerstman, Larry Ellison, Jim Sinegal, John Sperling, Mark Stevenson, Anand Nallathambi, Thomas Barrack, Jr., and many other innovators and leaders that I have met and gained mightily from doing so.

Thanks to Ed Trainor, Kevin Anderson, James Hickey, Wendell Jones, Ken Harris, DuWayne Peterson, Mike Brown, Jim Thornton, Abhi Beniwal, Al Biland, John Nomura, Eliot Weinman, John Desmond, and many others for their unwavering support during my career.

And most of all thanks as always to Lauren and Michael, for their ongoing support and for having seen me writing and heard much of this material during the many months involved in writing it. To their patience and willingness to listen.

INTRODUCTION

This is a book that provides the newest innovations and the latest Artificial Intelligence (AI) advances about the emerging nature of AI-based autonomous self-driving driverless cars. Via recent advances in Artificial Intelligence (AI) and Machine Learning (ML), we are nearing the day when vehicles can control themselves and will not require and nor rely upon human intervention to perform their driving tasks (or, that <u>allow</u> for human intervention, but only *require* human intervention in very limited ways).

Similar to my other related books, which I describe in a moment and list the chapters in the Appendix A of this book, I am particularly focused on those advances that pertain to self-driving cars. The phrase "autonomous vehicles" is often used to refer to any kind of vehicle, whether it is ground-based or in the air or sea, and whether it is a cargo hauling trailer truck or a conventional passenger car. Though the aspects described in this book are certainly applicable to all kinds of autonomous vehicles, I am focused more so here on cars.

Indeed, I am especially known for my role in aiding the advancement of self-driving cars, serving currently as the Executive Director of the Cybernetic AI Self-Driving Cars Institute. In addition to writing software, designing and developing systems and software for self-driving cars, I also speak and write quite a bit about the topic. This book is a collection of some of my more advanced essays. For those of you that might have seen my essays posted elsewhere, I have updated them and integrated them into this book as one handy cohesive package.

You might be interested in companion books that I have written that provide additional key innovations and fundamentals about self-driving cars. Those books are entitled **"Introduction to Driverless Self-Driving Cars,"** **"Advances in AI and Autonomous Vehicles: Cybernetic Self-Driving Cars,"** **"Self-Driving Cars: "The Mother of All AI Projects,"** **"Innovation and Thought Leadership on Self-Driving Driverless Cars,"** **"New Advances in AI Autonomous Driverless Self-Driving Cars,"** **"Autonomous Vehicle Driverless Self-Driving Cars and Artificial Intelligence,"** **"Transformative Artificial Intelligence**

Driverless Self-Driving Cars," "Disruptive Artificial Intelligence and Driverless Self-Driving Cars, and "State-of-the-Art AI Driverless Self-Driving Cars," and "Top Trends in AI Self-Driving Cars," and "AI Innovations and Self-Driving Cars," "Crucial Advances for AI Driverless Cars," "Sociotechnical Insights and AI Driverless Cars," "Pioneering Advances for AI Driverless Cars" and "Leading Edge Trends for AI Driverless Cars," "The Cutting Edge of AI Autonomous Cars" and "The Next Wave of AI Self-Driving Cars" and "Revolutionary Innovations of AI Self-Driving Cars," and "AI Self-Driving Cars Breakthroughs," "Trailblazing Trends for AI Self-Driving Cars," "Ingenious Strides for AI Driverless Cars," "AI Self-Driving Cars Inventiveness," "Visionary Secrets of AI Driverless Cars," "Spearheading AI Self-Driving Cars," "Spurring AI Self-Driving Cars," "Avant-Garde AI Driverless Cars," "AI Self-Driving Cars Evolvement," "AI Driverless Cars Chrysalis," "Boosting AI Autonomous Cars," "AI Self-Driving Cars Trendsetting," "AI Autonomous Cars Forefront, "AI Autonomous Cars Emergence," "AI Autonomous Cars Progress," "AI Self-Driving Cars Prognosis," "AI Self-Driving Cars Momentum," "AI Self-Driving Cars Headway," "AI Self-Driving Cars Vicissitude," "AI Self-Driving Cars Autonomy," "AI Driverless Cars Transmutation," "AI Driverless Cars Potentiality," "AI Driverless Cars Realities" (they are available on Amazon).

For this book, I am going to borrow my introduction from those companion books, since it does a good job of laying out the landscape of self-driving cars and my overall viewpoints on the topic. The remainder of this book is material that does not appear in the companion books.

INTRODUCTION TO SELF-DRIVING CARS

This is a book about self-driving cars. Someday in the future, we'll all have self-driving cars and this book will perhaps seem antiquated, but right now, we are at the forefront of the self-driving car wave. Daily news bombards us with flashes of new announcements by one car maker or another and leaves the impression that within the next few weeks or maybe months that the self-driving car will be here. A casual non-technical reader would assume from these news flashes that in fact we must be on the cusp of a true self-driving car. We are still quite a distance from having a true self-driving car.

A true self-driving car is akin to a moonshot. In the same manner that getting us to the moon was an incredible feat, likewise, is achieving a true self-driving car. Anybody that suggests or even brashly states that the true self-driving car is nearly here should be viewed with great skepticism. Indeed, you'll see that I often tend to use the word "hogwash" or "crock" when I assess much of the decidedly *fake news* about self-driving cars.

Indeed, I've been writing a popular blog post about self-driving cars and hitting hard on those that try to wave their hands and pretend that we are on the imminent verge of true self-driving cars. For many years, I've been known as the AI Insider. Besides writing about AI, I also develop AI software. I do what I describe. It also gives me insights into what others that are doing AI are really doing versus what it is said they are doing.

Many faithful readers had asked me to pull together my insightful short essays and put them into another book, which you are now holding.

For those of you that have been reading my essays over the years, this collection not only puts them together into one handy package, I also updated the essays and added new material. For those of you that are new to the topic of self-driving cars and AI, I hope you find these essays approachable and informative. I also tend to have a writing style with a bit of a voice, and so you'll see that I am times have a wry sense of humor and poke at conformity.

As a former professor and founder of an AI research lab, I for many years wrote in the formal language of academic writing. I published in referred journals and served as an editor for several AI journals. This writing here is not of the nature, and I have adopted a different and more informal style for these essays. That being said, I also do mention from time-to-time more rigorous material on AI and encourage you all to dig into those deeper and more formal materials if so interested.

I am also an AI practitioner. This means that I write AI software for a living. Currently, I head-up the Cybernetics Self-Driving Car Institute, where we are developing AI software for self-driving cars.

For those of you that are reading this book and have a penchant for writing code, you might consider taking a look at the open source code available for self-driving cars. This is a handy place to start learning how to develop AI for self-driving cars. There are also many new educational courses spring forth. There is a growing body of those wanting to learn about and develop self-driving cars, and a growing body of colleges, labs, and other avenues by which you can learn about self-driving cars.

This book will provide a foundation of aspects that I think will get you ready for those kinds of more advanced training opportunities. If you've already taken those classes, you'll likely find these essays especially interesting as they offer a perspective that I am betting few other instructors or faculty offered to you. These are challenging essays that ask you to think beyond the conventional about self-driving cars.

THE MOTHER OF ALL AI PROJECTS

In June 2017, Apple CEO Tim Cook came out and finally admitted that Apple has been working on a self-driving car. As you'll see in my essays, Apple was enmeshed in secrecy about their self-driving car efforts. We have only been able to read the tea leaves and guess at what Apple has been up to. The notion of an iCar has been floating for quite a while, and self-driving engineers and researchers have been signing tight-lipped Non-Disclosure Agreements (NDA's) to work on projects at Apple that were as shrouded in mystery as any military invasion plans might be.

Tim Cook said something that many others in the Artificial Intelligence (AI) field have been saying, namely, the creation of a self-driving car has got to be the mother of all AI projects. In other words, it is in fact a tremendous moonshot for AI. If a self-driving car can be crafted and the AI works as we hope, it means that we have made incredible strides with AI and that therefore it opens many other worlds of potential breakthrough accomplishments that AI can solve.

Is this hyperbole? Am I just trying to make AI seem like a miracle worker and so provide self-aggrandizing statements for those of us writing the AI software for self-driving cars? No, it is not hyperbole. Developing a true self-driving car is really, really, really hard to do. Let me take a moment to explain why. As a side note, I realize that the Apple CEO is known for at times uttering hyperbole, and he had previously said for example that the year 2012 was "the mother of all years," and he had said that the release of iOS 10 was "the mother of all releases" – all of which does suggest he likes to use the handy "mother of" expression. But, I assure you, in terms of true self-driving cars, he has hit the nail on the head. For sure.

When you think about a moonshot and how we got to the moon, there are some identifiable characteristics and those same aspects can be applied to creating a true self-driving car. You'll notice that I keep putting the word "true" in front of the self-driving car expression. I do so because as per my essay about the various levels of self-driving cars, there are some self-driving cars that are only somewhat of a self-driving car. The somewhat versions are ones that require a human driver to be ready to intervene. In my view, that's not a true self-driving car. A true self-driving car is one that requires no human driver intervention at all. It is a car that can entirely undertake via automation the driving task without any human driver needed. This is the essence of what is known as a Level 5 self-driving car. We are currently at the Level 2 and Level 3 mark, and not yet at Level 5.

Getting to the moon involved aspects such as having big stretch goals, incremental progress, experimentation, innovation, and so on. Let's review how this applied to the moonshot of the bygone era, and how it applies to the self-driving car moonshot of today.

Big Stretch Goal

Trying to take a human and deliver the human to the moon, and bring them back, safely, was an extremely large stretch goal at the time. No one knew whether it could be done. The technology wasn't available yet. The cost was huge. The determination would need to be fierce. Etc. To reach a Level 5 self-driving car is going to be the same. It is a big stretch goal. We can readily get to the Level 3, and we are able to see the Level 4 just up ahead, but a Level 5 is still an unknown as to if it is doable. It should eventually be doable and in the same way that we thought we'd eventually get to the moon, but when it will occur is a different story.

Incremental Progress

Getting to the moon did not happen overnight in one fell swoop. It took years and years of incremental progress to get there. Likewise for self-driving cars. Google has famously been striving to get to the Level 5, and pretty much been willing to forgo dealing with the intervening levels, but most of the other self-driving car makers are doing the incremental route. Let's get a good Level 2 and a somewhat Level 3 going. Then, let's improve the Level 3 and get a somewhat Level 4 going. Then, let's improve the Level 4 and finally arrive at a Level 5. This seems to be the prevalent way that we are going to achieve the true self-driving car.

Experimentation

You likely know that there were various experiments involved in perfecting the approach and technology to get to the moon. As per making incremental progress, we first tried to see if we could get a rocket to go into space and safety return, then put a monkey in there, then with a human, then we went all the way to the moon but didn't land, and finally we arrived at the mission that actually landed on the moon. Self-driving cars are the same way. We are doing simulations of self-driving cars. We do testing of self-driving cars on private land under controlled situations. We do testing of self-driving cars on public roadways, often having to meet regulatory requirements including for example having an engineer or equivalent in the car to take over the controls if needed. And so on. Experiments big and small are needed to figure out what works and what doesn't.

Innovation

There are already some advances in AI that are allowing us to progress toward self-driving cars. We are going to need even more advances. Innovation in all aspects of technology are going to be required to achieve a true self-driving car. By no means do we already have everything in-hand that we need to get there. Expect new inventions and new approaches, new algorithms, etc.

Setbacks

Most of the pundits are avoiding talking about potential setbacks in the progress toward self-driving cars. Getting to the moon involved many setbacks, some of which you never have heard of and were buried at the time so as to not dampen enthusiasm and funding for getting to the moon. A recurring theme in many of my included essays is that there are going to be setbacks as we try to arrive at a true self-driving car. Take a deep breath and be ready. I just hope the setbacks don't completely stop progress. I am sure that it will cause progress to alter in a manner that we've not yet seen in the self-driving car field. I liken the self-driving car of today to the excitement everyone had for Uber when it first got going. Today, we have a different view of Uber and with each passing day there are more regulations to the ride sharing business and more concerns raised. The darling child only stays a darling until finally that child acts up. It will happen the same with self-driving cars.

SELF-DRIVING CARS CHALLENGES

But what exactly makes things so hard to have a true self-driving car, you might be asking. You have seen cruise control for years and years. You've lately seen cars that can do parallel parking. You've seen YouTube videos of Tesla drivers that put their hands out the window as their car zooms along the highway, and seen to therefore be in a self-driving car. Aren't we just needing to put a few more sensors onto a car and then we'll have in-hand a true self-driving car? Nope.

Consider for a moment the nature of the driving task. We don't just let anyone at any age drive a car. Worldwide, most countries won't license a driver until the age of 18, though many do allow a learner's permit at the age of 15 or 16. Some suggest that a younger age would be physically too small to reach the controls of the car. Though this might be the case, we could easily adjust the controls to allow for younger aged and thus smaller stature.

It's not their physical size that matters. It's their cognitive development that matters.

To drive a car, you need to be able to reason about the car, what the car can and cannot do. You need to know how to operate the car. You need to know about how other cars on the road drive. You need to know what is allowed in driving such as speed limits and driving within marked lanes. You need to be able to react to situations and be able to avoid getting into accidents. You need to ascertain when to hit your brakes, when to steer clear of a pedestrian, and how to keep from ramming that motorcyclist that just cut you off.

Many of us had taken courses on driving. We studied about driving and took driver training. We had to take a test and pass it to be able to drive. The point being that though most adults take the driving task for granted, and we often "mindlessly" drive our cars, there is a significant amount of cognitive effort that goes into driving a car. After a while, it becomes second nature. You don't especially think about how you drive, you just do it. But, if you watch a novice driver, say a teenager learning to drive, you suddenly realize that there is a lot more complexity to it than we seem to realize.

Furthermore, driving is a very serious task. I recall when my daughter and son first learned to drive. They are both very conscientious people. They wanted to make sure that whatever they did, they did well, and that they did not harm anyone. Every day, when you get into a car, it is probably around 4,000 pounds of hefty metal and plastics (about two tons), and it is a lethal weapon. Think about it. You drive down the street in an object that weighs two tons and with the engine it can accelerate and ram into anything you want to hit. The damage a car can inflict is very scary. Both my children were surprised that they were being given the right to maneuver this monster of a beast that could cause tremendous harm entirely by merely letting go of the steering wheel for a moment or taking your eyes off the road.

In fact, in the United States alone there are about 30,000 deaths per year by auto accidents, which is around 100 per day. Given that there are about 263 million cars in the United States, I am actually more amazed that the number of fatalities is not a lot higher. During my morning commute, I look at all the thousands of cars on the freeway around me, and I think that if all of them decided to go zombie and drive in a crazy maniac way, there would be many people dead. Somehow, incredibly, each day, most people drive relatively safely. To me, that's a miracle right there. Getting millions and millions of people to be safe and sane when behind the wheel of a two ton mobile object, it's a feat that we as a society should admire with pride.

So, hopefully you are in agreement that the driving task requires a great deal of cognition. You don't' need to be especially smart to drive a car, and we've done quite a bit to make car driving viable for even the average dolt. There isn't an IQ test that you need to take to drive a car. If you can read and write, and pass a test, you pretty much can legally drive a car. There are of course some that drive a car and are not legally permitted to do so, plus there are private areas such as farms where drivers are young, but for public roadways in the United States, you can be generally of average intelligence (or less) and be able to legally drive.

This though makes it seem like the cognitive effort must not be much. If the cognitive effort was truly hard, wouldn't we only have Einstein's that could drive a car? We have made sure to keep the driving task as simple as we can, by making the controls easy and relatively standardized, and by having roads that are relatively standardized, and so on. It is as though Disneyland has put their Autopia into the real-world, by us all as a society agreeing that roads will be a certain way, and we'll all abide by the various rules of driving.

A modest cognitive task by a human is still something that stymies AI. You certainly know that AI has been able to beat chess players and be good at other kinds of games. This type of narrow cognition is not what car driving is about. Car driving is much wider. It requires knowledge about the world, which a chess playing AI system does not need to know. The cognitive aspects of driving are on the one hand seemingly simple, but at the same time require layer upon layer of knowledge about cars, people, roads, rules, and a myriad of other "common sense" aspects. We don't have any AI systems today that have that same kind of breadth and depth of awareness and knowledge.

As revealed in my essays, the self-driving car of today is using trickery to do particular tasks. It is all very narrow in operation. Plus, it currently assumes that a human driver is ready to intervene. It is like a child that we have taught to stack blocks, but we are needed to be right there in case the child stacks them too high and they begin to fall over. AI of today is brittle, it is narrow, and it does not approach the cognitive abilities of humans. This is why the true self-driving car is somewhere out in the future.

Another aspect to the driving task is that it is not solely a mind exercise. You do need to use your senses to drive. You use your eyes a vision sensors to see the road ahead. You vision capability is like a streaming video, which your brain needs to continually analyze as you drive. Where is the road? Is there a pedestrian in the way? Is there another car ahead of you? Your senses are relying a flood of info to your brain. Self-driving cars are trying to do the same, by using cameras, radar, ultrasound, and lasers. This is an attempt at mimicking how humans have senses and sensory apparatus.

Thus, the driving task is mental and physical. You use your senses, you use your arms and legs to manipulate the controls of the car, and you use your brain to assess the sensory info and direct your limbs to act upon the controls of the car. This all happens instantly. If you've ever perhaps gotten something in your eye and only had one eye available to drive with, you suddenly realize how dependent upon vision you are. If you have a broken foot with a cast, you suddenly realize how hard it is to control the brake pedal and the accelerator. If you've taken medication and your brain is maybe sluggish, you suddenly realize how much mental strain is required to drive a car.

An AI system that plays chess only needs to be focused on playing chess. The physical aspects aren't important because usually a human moves the chess pieces or the chessboard is shown on an electronic display. Using AI for a more life-and-death task such as analyzing MRI images of patients, this again does not require physical capabilities and instead is done by examining images of bits.

Driving a car is a true life-and-death task. It is a use of AI that can easily and at any moment produce death. For those colleagues of mine that are developing this AI, as am I, we need to keep in mind the somber aspects of this. We are producing software that will have in its virtual hands the lives of the occupants of the car, and the lives of those in other nearby cars, and the lives of nearby pedestrians, etc. Chess is not usually a life-or-death matter.

Driving is all around us. Cars are everywhere. Most of today's AI applications involve only a small number of people. Or, they are behind the scenes and we as humans have other recourse if the AI messes up. AI that is driving a car at 80 miles per hour on a highway had better not mess up. The consequences are grave. Multiply this by the number of cars, if we could put magically self-driving into every car in the USA, we'd have AI running in the 263 million cars. That's a lot of AI spread around. This is AI on a massive scale that we are not doing today and that offers both promise and potential peril.

There are some that want AI for self-driving cars because they envision a world without any car accidents. They envision a world in which there is no car congestion and all cars cooperate with each other. These are wonderful utopian visions.

They are also very misleading. The adoption of self-driving cars is going to be incremental and not overnight. We cannot economically just junk all existing cars. Nor are we going to be able to affordably retrofit existing cars. It is more likely that self-driving cars will be built into new cars and that over many years of gradual replacement of existing cars that we'll see the mix of self-driving cars become substantial in the real-world.

In these essays, I have tried to offer technological insights without being overly technical in my description, and also blended the business, societal, and economic aspects too. Technologists need to consider the non-technological impacts of what they do. Non-technologists should be aware of what is being developed.

We all need to work together to collectively be prepared for the enormous disruption and transformative aspects of true self-driving cars.

WHAT THIS BOOK PROVIDES

What does this book provide to you? It introduces many of the key elements about self-driving cars and does so with an AI based perspective. I weave together technical and non-technical aspects, readily going from being concerned about the cognitive capabilities of the driving task and how the technology is embodying this into self-driving cars, and in the next breath I discuss the societal and economic aspects.

They are all intertwined because that's the way reality is. You cannot separate out the technology per se, and instead must consider it within the milieu of what is being invented and innovated, and do so with a mindset towards the contemporary mores and culture that shape what we are doing and what we hope to do.

WHY THIS BOOK

I wrote this book to try and bring to the public view many aspects about self-driving cars that nobody seems to be discussing.

For business leaders that are either involved in making self-driving cars or that are going to leverage self-driving cars, I hope that this book will enlighten you as to the risks involved and ways in which you should be strategizing about how to deal with those risks.

For entrepreneurs, startups and other businesses that want to enter into the self-driving car market that is emerging, I hope this book sparks your interest in doing so, and provides some sense of what might be prudent to pursue.

For researchers that study self-driving cars, I hope this book spurs your interest in the risks and safety issues of self-driving cars, and also nudges you toward conducting research on those aspects.

For students in computer science or related disciplines, I hope this book will provide you with interesting and new ideas and material, for which you might conduct research or provide some career direction insights for you.

For AI companies and high-tech companies pursuing self-driving cars, this book will hopefully broaden your view beyond just the mere coding and development needed to make self-driving cars.

For all readers, I hope that you will find the material in this book to be stimulating. Some of it will be repetitive of things you already know. But I am pretty sure that you'll also find various eureka moments whereby you'll discover a new technique or approach that you had not earlier thought of. I am also betting that there will be material that forces you to rethink some of your current practices.

I am not saying you will suddenly have an epiphany and change what you are doing. I do think though that you will reconsider or perhaps revisit what you are doing.

For anyone choosing to use this book for teaching purposes, please take a look at my suggestions for doing so, as described in the Appendix. I have found the material handy in courses that I have taught, and likewise other faculty have told me that they have found the material handy, in some cases as extended readings and in other instances as a core part of their course (depending on the nature of the class).

In my writing for this book, I have tried carefully to blend both the practitioner and the academic styles of writing. It is not as dense as is typical academic journal writing, but at the same time offers depth by going into the nuances and trade-offs of various practices.

The word "deep" is in vogue today, meaning getting deeply into a subject or topic, and so is the word "unpack" which means to tease out the underlying aspects of a subject or topic. I have sought to offer material that addresses an issue or topic by going relatively deeply into it and make sure that it is well unpacked.

In any book about AI, it is difficult to use our everyday words without having some of them be misinterpreted. Specifically, it is easy to anthropomorphize AI. When I say that an AI system "knows" something, I do not want you to construe that the AI system has sentience and "knows" in the same way that humans do. They aren't that way, as yet. I have tried to use quotes around such words from time-to-time to emphasize that the words I am using should not be misinterpreted to ascribe true human intelligence to the AI systems that we know of today. If I used quotes around all such words, the book would be very difficult to read, and so I am doing so judiciously. Please keep that in mind as you read the material, thanks.

Some of the material is time-based in terms of covering underway activities, and though some of it might decay, nonetheless I believe you'll find the material useful and informative.

COMPANION BOOKS

1. "Introduction to Driverless Self-Driving Cars" by Dr. Lance Eliot
2. "Innovation and Thought Leadership on Self-Driving Driverless Cars" by Dr. Lance Eliot
3. "Advances in AI and Autonomous Vehicles: Cybernetic Self-Driving Cars" by Dr. Lance Eliot
4. "Self-Driving Cars: The Mother of All AI Projects" by Dr. Lance Eliot
5. "New Advances in AI Autonomous Driverless Self-Driving Cars" by Dr. Lance Eliot
6. "Autonomous Vehicle Driverless Self-Driving Cars and Artificial Intelligence" by Dr. Lance Eliot and Michael B. Eliot
7. "Transformative Artificial Intelligence Driverless Self-Driving Cars" by Dr. Lance Eliot
8. "Disruptive Artificial Intelligence and Driverless Self-Driving Cars" by Dr. Lance Eliot
9. "State-of-the-Art AI Driverless Self-Driving Cars" by Dr. Lance Eliot
10. "Top Trends in AI Self-Driving Cars" by Dr. Lance Eliot
11. "AI Innovations and Self-Driving Cars" by Dr. Lance Eliot
12. "Crucial Advances for AI Driverless Cars" by Dr. Lance Eliot
13. "Sociotechnical Insights and AI Driverless Cars" by Dr. Lance Eliot.
14. "Pioneering Advances for AI Driverless Cars" by Dr. Lance Eliot
15. "Leading Edge Trends for AI Driverless Cars" by Dr. Lance Eliot
16. "The Cutting Edge of AI Autonomous Cars" by Dr. Lance Eliot
17. "The Next Wave of AI Self-Driving Cars" by Dr. Lance Eliot
18. "Revolutionary Innovations of AI Driverless Cars" by Dr. Lance Eliot
19. "AI Self-Driving Cars Breakthroughs" by Dr. Lance Eliot
20. "Trailblazing Trends for AI Self-Driving Cars" by Dr. Lance Eliot
21. "Ingenious Strides for AI Driverless Cars" by Dr. Lance Eliot
22. "AI Self-Driving Cars Inventiveness" by Dr. Lance Eliot
23. "Visionary Secrets of AI Driverless Cars" by Dr. Lance Eliot
24. "Spearheading AI Self-Driving Cars" by Dr. Lance Eliot
25. "Spurring AI Self-Driving Cars" by Dr. Lance Eliot
26. "Avant-Garde AI Driverless Cars" by Dr. Lance Eliot
27. "AI Self-Driving Cars Evolvement" by Dr. Lance Eliot
28. "AI Driverless Cars Chrysalis" by Dr. Lance Eliot
29. "Boosting AI Autonomous Cars" by Dr. Lance Eliot
30. "AI Self-Driving Cars Trendsetting" by Dr. Lance Eliot
31. "AI Autonomous Cars Forefront" by Dr. Lance Eliot
32. "AI Autonomous Cars Emergence" by Dr. Lance Eliot
33. "AI Autonomous Cars Progress" by Dr. Lance Eliot
34. "AI Self-Driving Cars Prognosis" by Dr. Lance Eliot
35. "AI Self-Driving Cars Momentum" by Dr. Lance Eliot
36. "AI Self-Driving Cars Headway" by Dr. Lance Eliot
37. "AI Self-Driving Cars Vicissitude" by Dr. Lance Eliot
38. "AI Self-Driving Cars Autonomy" by Dr. Lance Eliot
39. "AI Driverless Cars Transmutation" by Dr. Lance Eliot
40. "AI Driverless Cars Potentiality" by Dr. Lance Eliot
41. "AI Driverless Cars Realities" by Dr. Lance Eliot

These books are available on Amazon and at other major global booksellers.

CHAPTER 1

ELIOT FRAMEWORK FOR AI SELF-DRIVING CARS

`

CHAPTER 1

ELIOT FRAMEWORK FOR
AI SELF-DRIVING CARS

This chapter is a core foundational aspect for understanding AI self-driving cars and I have used this same chapter in several of my other books to introduce the reader to essential elements of this field. Once you've read this chapter, you'll be prepared to read the rest of the material since the foundational essence of the components of autonomous AI driverless self-driving cars will have been established for you.

When I give presentations about self-driving cars and teach classes on the topic, I have found it helpful to provide a framework around which the various key elements of self-driving cars can be understood and organized (see diagram at the end of this chapter). The framework needs to be simple enough to convey the overarching elements, but at the same time not so simple that it belies the true complexity of self-driving cars. As such, I am going to describe the framework here and try to offer in a thousand words (or more!) what the framework diagram itself intends to portray.

The core elements on the diagram are numbered for ease of reference. The numbering does not suggest any kind of prioritization of the elements. Each element is crucial. Each element has a purpose, and otherwise would not be included in the framework. For some self-driving cars, a particular element might be more important or somehow distinguished in comparison to other self-driving cars.

You could even use the framework to rate a particular self-driving car, doing so by gauging how well it performs in each of the elements of the framework. I will describe each of the elements, one at a time. After doing so, I'll discuss aspects that illustrate how the elements interact and perform during the overall effort of a self-driving car.

At the Cybernetic Self-Driving Car Institute, we use the framework to keep track of what we are working on, and how we are developing software that fills in what is needed to achieve Level 5 self-driving cars.

D-01: Sensor Capture

Let's start with the one element that often gets the most attention in the press about self-driving cars, namely, the sensory devices for a self-driving car.

On the framework, the box labeled as D-01 indicates "Sensor Capture" and refers to the processes of the self-driving car that involve collecting data from the myriad of sensors that are used for a self-driving car. The types of devices typically involved are listed, such as the use of mono cameras, stereo cameras, LIDAR devices, radar systems, ultrasonic devices, GPS, IMU, and so on.

These devices are tasked with obtaining data about the status of the self-driving car and the world around it. Some of the devices are continually providing updates, while others of the devices await an indication by the self-driving car that the device is supposed to collect data. The data might be first transformed in some fashion by the device itself, or it might instead be fed directly into the sensor capture as raw data. At that point, it might be up to the sensor capture processes to do transformations on the data. This all varies depending upon the nature of the devices being used and how the devices were designed and developed.

D-02: Sensor Fusion

Imagine that your eyeballs receive visual images, your nose receives odors, your ears receive sounds, and in essence each of your distinct sensory devices is getting some form of input. The input befits the nature of the device. Likewise, for a self-driving car, the cameras provide visual images, the radar returns radar reflections, and so on.

Each device provides the data as befits what the device does.

At some point, using the analogy to humans, you need to merge together what your eyes see, what your nose smells, what your ears hear, and piece it all together into a larger sense of what the world is all about and what is happening around you. Sensor fusion is the action of taking the singular aspects from each of the devices and putting them together into a larger puzzle.

Sensor fusion is a tough task. There are some devices that might not be working at the time of the sensor capture. Or, there might some devices that are unable to report well what they have detected. Again, using a human analogy, suppose you are in a dark room and so your eyes cannot see much. At that point, you might need to rely more so on your ears and what you hear. The same is true for a self-driving car. If the cameras are obscured due to snow and sleet, it might be that the radar can provide a greater indication of what the external conditions consist of.

In the case of a self-driving car, there can be a plethora of such sensory devices. Each is reporting what it can. Each might have its difficulties. Each might have its limitations, such as how far ahead it can detect an object. All of these limitations need to be considered during the sensor fusion task.

D-03: Virtual World Model

For humans, we presumably keep in our minds a model of the world around us when we are driving a car. In your mind, you know that the car is going at say 60 miles per hour and that you are on a freeway. You have a model in your mind that your car is surrounded by other cars, and that there are lanes to the freeway. Your model is not only based on what you can see, hear, etc., but also what you know about the nature of the world. You know that at any moment that car ahead of you can smash on its brakes, or the car behind you can ram into your car, or that the truck in the next lane might swerve into your lane.

The AI of the self-driving car needs to have a virtual world model, which it then keeps updated with whatever it is receiving from the sensor fusion, which received its input from the sensor capture and the sensory devices.

D-04: System Action Plan

By having a virtual world model, the AI of the self-driving car is able to keep track of where the car is and what is happening around the car. In addition, the AI needs to determine what to do next. Should the self-driving car hit its brakes? Should the self-driving car stay in its lane or swerve into the lane to the left? Should the self-driving car accelerate or slow down?

A system action plan needs to be prepared by the AI of the self-driving car. The action plan specifies what actions should be taken. The actions need to pertain to the status of the virtual world model. Plus, the actions need to be realizable.

This realizability means that the AI cannot just assert that the self-driving car should suddenly sprout wings and fly. Instead, the AI must be bound by whatever the self-driving car can actually do, such as coming to a halt in a distance of X feet at a speed of Y miles per hour, rather than perhaps asserting that the self-driving car come to a halt in 0 feet as though it could instantaneously come to a stop while it is in motion.

D-05: Controls Activation

The system action plan is implemented by activating the controls of the car to act according to what the plan stipulates. This might mean that the accelerator control is commanded to increase the speed of the car. Or, the steering control is commanded to turn the steering wheel 30 degrees to the left or right.

One question arises as to whether or not the controls respond as they are commanded to do. In other words, suppose the AI has commanded the accelerator to increase, but for some reason it does not do so. Or, maybe it tries to do so, but the speed of the car does not increase. The controls activation feeds back into the virtual world model, and simultaneously the virtual world model is getting updated from the sensors, the sensor capture, and the sensor fusion. This allows the AI to ascertain what has taken place as a result of the controls being commanded to take some kind of action.

By the way, please keep in mind that though the diagram seems to have a linear progression to it, the reality is that these are all aspects of the self-driving car that are happening in parallel and simultaneously. The sensors are capturing data, meanwhile the sensor fusion is taking place, meanwhile the virtual model is being updated, meanwhile the system action plan is being formulated and reformulated, meanwhile the controls are being activated.

This is the same as a human being that is driving a car. They are eyeballing the road, meanwhile they are fusing in their mind the sights, sounds, etc., meanwhile their mind is updating their model of the world around them, meanwhile they are formulating an action plan of what to do, and meanwhile they are pushing their foot onto the pedals and steering the car. In the normal course of driving a car, you are doing all of these at once. I mention this so that when you look at the diagram, you will think of the boxes as processes that are all happening at the same time, and not as though only one happens and then the next.

They are shown diagrammatically in a simplistic manner to help comprehend what is taking place. You though should also realize that they are working in parallel and simultaneous with each other. This is a tough aspect in that the inter-element communications involve latency and other aspects that must be taken into account. There can be delays in one element updating and then sharing its latest status with other elements.

D-06: Automobile & CAN

Contemporary cars use various automotive electronics and a Controller Area Network (CAN) to serve as the components that underlie the driving aspects of a car. There are Electronic Control Units (ECU's) which control subsystems of the car, such as the engine, the brakes, the doors, the windows, and so on.

The elements D-01, D-02, D-03, D-04, D-05 are layered on top of the D-06, and must be aware of the nature of what the D-06 is able to do and not do.

D-07: In-Car Commands

Humans are going to be occupants in self-driving cars. In a Level 5 self-driving car, there must be some form of communication that takes place between the humans and the self-driving car. For example, I go into a self-driving car and tell it that I want to be driven over to Disneyland, and along the way I want to stop at In-and-Out Burger. The self-driving car now parses what I've said and tries to then establish a means to carry out my wishes.

In-car commands can happen at any time during a driving journey. Though my example was about an in-car command when I first got into my self-driving car, it could be that while the self-driving car is carrying out the journey that I change my mind. Perhaps after getting stuck in traffic, I tell the self-driving car to forget about getting the burgers and just head straight over to the theme park. The self-driving car needs to be alert to in-car commands throughout the journey.

D-08: V2X Communications

We will ultimately have self-driving cars communicating with each other, doing so via V2V (Vehicle-to-Vehicle) communications. We will also have self-driving cars that communicate with the roadways and other aspects of the transportation infrastructure, doing so via V2I (Vehicle-to-Infrastructure).

The variety of ways in which a self-driving car will be communicating with other cars and infrastructure is being called V2X, whereby the letter X means whatever else we identify as something that a car should or would want to communicate with. The V2X communications will be taking place simultaneous with everything else on the diagram, and those other elements will need to incorporate whatever it gleans from those V2X communications.

D-09: Deep Learning

The use of Deep Learning permeates all other aspects of the self-driving car. The AI of the self-driving car will be using deep learning to do a better job at the systems action plan, and at the controls activation, and at the sensor fusion, and so on.

Currently, the use of artificial neural networks is the most prevalent form of deep learning. Based on large swaths of data, the neural networks attempt to "learn" from the data and therefore direct the efforts of the self-driving car accordingly.

D-10: Tactical AI

Tactical AI is the element of dealing with the moment-to-moment driving of the self-driving car. Is the self-driving car staying in its lane of the freeway? Is the car responding appropriately to the controls commands? Are the sensory devices working?

For human drivers, the tactical equivalent can be seen when you watch a novice driver such as a teenager that is first driving. They are focused on the mechanics of the driving task, keeping their eye on the road while also trying to properly control the car.

D-11: Strategic AI

The Strategic AI aspects of a self-driving car are dealing with the larger picture of what the self-driving car is trying to do. If I had asked that the self-driving car take me to Disneyland, there is an overall journey map that needs to be kept and maintained.

There is an interaction between the Strategic AI and the Tactical AI. The Strategic AI is wanting to keep on the mission of the driving, while the Tactical AI is focused on the particulars underway in the driving effort. If the Tactical AI seems to wander away from the overarching mission, the Strategic AI wants to see why and get things back on track. If the Tactical AI realizes that there is something amiss on the self-driving car, it needs to alert the Strategic AI accordingly and have an adjustment to the overarching mission that is underway.

D-12: Self-Aware AI

Very few of the self-driving cars being developed are including a Self-Aware AI element, which we at the Cybernetic Self-Driving Car Institute believe is crucial to Level 5 self-driving cars.

The Self-Aware AI element is intended to watch over itself, in the sense that the AI is making sure that the AI is working as intended. Suppose you had a human driving a car, and they were starting to drive erratically. Hopefully, their own self-awareness would make them realize they themselves are driving poorly, such as perhaps starting to fall asleep after having been driving for hours on end. If you had a passenger in the car, they might be able to alert the driver if the driver is starting to do something amiss. This is exactly what the Self-Aware

AI element tries to do, it becomes the overseer of the AI, and tries to detect when the AI has become faulty or confused, and then find ways to overcome the issue.

D-13: Economic

The economic aspects of a self-driving car are not per se a technology aspect of a self-driving car, but the economics do indeed impact the nature of a self-driving car. For example, the cost of outfitting a self-driving car with every kind of possible sensory device is prohibitive, and so choices need to be made about which devices are used. And, for those sensory devices chosen, whether they would have a full set of features or a more limited set of features.

We are going to have self-driving cars that are at the low-end of a consumer cost point, and others at the high-end of a consumer cost point. You cannot expect that the self-driving car at the low-end is going to be as robust as the one at the high-end. I realize that many of the self-driving car pundits are acting as though all self-driving cars will be the same, but they won't be. Just like anything else, we are going to have self-driving cars that have a range of capabilities. Some will be better than others. Some will be safer than others. This is the way of the real-world, and so we need to be thinking about the economics aspects when considering the nature of self-driving cars.

D-14: Societal

This component encompasses the societal aspects of AI which also impacts the technology of self-driving cars. For example, the famous Trolley Problem involves what choices should a self-driving car make when faced with life-and-death matters. If the self-driving car is about to either hit a child standing in the roadway, or instead ram into a tree at the side of the road and possibly kill the humans in the self-driving car, which choice should be made?

We need to keep in mind the societal aspects will underlie the AI of the self-driving car. Whether we are aware of it explicitly or not, the AI will have embedded into it various societal assumptions.

D-15: Innovation

I included the notion of innovation into the framework because we can anticipate that whatever a self-driving car consists of, it will continue to be innovated over time. The self-driving cars coming out in the next several years will undoubtedly be different and less innovative than the versions that come out in ten years hence, and so on.

Framework Overall

For those of you that want to learn about self-driving cars, you can potentially pick a particular element and become specialized in that aspect. Some engineers are focusing on the sensory devices. Some engineers focus on the controls activation. And so on. There are specialties in each of the elements.

Researchers are likewise specializing in various aspects. For example, there are researchers that are using Deep Learning to see how best it can be used for sensor fusion. There are other researchers that are using Deep Learning to derive good System Action Plans. Some are studying how to develop AI for the Strategic aspects of the driving task, while others are focused on the Tactical aspects.

A well-prepared all-around software developer that is involved in self-driving cars should be familiar with all of the elements, at least to the degree that they know what each element does. This is important since whatever piece of the pie that the software developer works on, they need to be knowledgeable about what the other elements are doing.

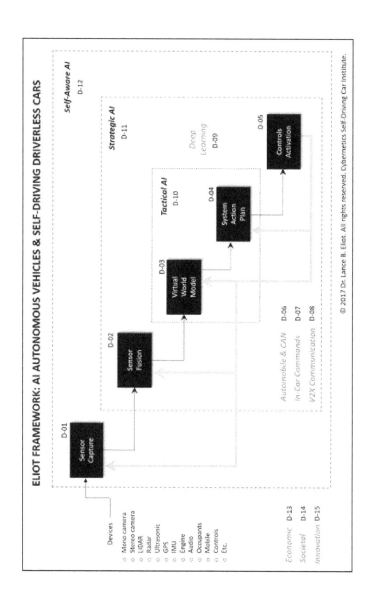

CHAPTER 2
NON-DRIVING ROBOTS
AND
AI SELF-DRIVING CARS

CHAPTER 2

NON-DRIVING ROBOTS AND AI SELF-DRIVING CARS

A ridesharing driver the other day aided a passenger that had a leg cast to get into his car.

A mother recently helped her toddler put on a seatbelt and held the hand of her child while taking a short driving journey.

These two everyday occurrences are seemingly innocuous and would not normally merit explicitly being pointed out.

They are noteworthy when you consider the underlying element that runs in-common among these use cases, namely, passengers often require assistance while traveling via a car.

Let's refer to this assistance as a helping hand.

You might need a helping hand to get into a car.

You might need a helping hand when trying to exit from a car.

At times, during a car journey, you might need a helping hand.

With today's cars, there is always a human driver at the wheel and therefore a potential helping hand is already baked into car travel.

The driver can possibly get out of the car to open a car door for someone or aid a person to get into the car or offer help while a person is aiming to get out of a car.

In addition, while sitting at the steering wheel, a driver can reach over to provide a limited amount of assistance, though hopefully doing so in a careful way to ensure that their attention is still focused on the driving task. When a car comes up to a red light and assuming that the driver has brought the car to a full and safe stop, the driver can be more lax in their driving focus, allowing them to provide greater assistance within the car, yet presumably still in control of the vehicle.

For true self-driving cars, there won't be a human driver at the wheel.

All occupants inside a true self-driving car are passengers. And, if there is only one person in a self-driving car, it means they are the only passenger and there isn't anyone else present. This is an important point. In today's conventional cars, when there is one passenger there is also another person in the car that's the driver of the car.

The significance of not having a human driver in a car means that no longer will passengers have another human readily at hand that can help them while undertaking car travel.

This is an aspect that we today take for granted and assume that the driver will be available in some manner to help. Sure, some drivers might be grumpy and hesitant to offer a helping hand, and in fact the surly drivers might refuse outright to assist. Overall, it seems that most drivers would be willing to assist another human that is a passenger, despite the reality that a few drivers might not.

The subtle availability of a helping hand is generally hidden from view and none of us tend to think about the utility of this crucial aspect.

Only when you struggle to get into or out of a car would you suddenly be aware of the need to seek assistance and leverage the driver as a helping hand. Likewise, if you have difficulty putting on a seatbelt, only then might the driver's helping assistance come to play as they reach over to aid in getting your seat buckled.

Once we have a prevalence of true self-driving cars, I predict that we will all have a revelation that the helping hand has disappeared.

Indeed, in a prior posting, I've suggested that we might see the emergence of a kind of nanny or concierge role for aiding people that opt to use self-driving cars. When you request a ridesharing car, and if it is a self-driving car, you might indicate that you also want to have a helping hand provided in the vehicle.

The helping hand would be a person that is along for the ride and does so to assist the passenger that will be using the self-driving car.

Keep in mind that the person providing this helping hand does not need to know how to drive and in fact, won't be driving the car. AI is driving the car. The purpose of the ride-along person is to help any passenger that might need some form of physical assistance of getting into, out of, or needs help during the journey.

Presumably, ridesharing services will charge an extra fee for passengers that request a ride-along assistant. Or, it could become a competitive differentiator among ridesharing services that employ self-driving cars, of which some ridesharing firms might provide a free helping hand as a marketing strategy to get passengers to use their ridesharing driverless cars versus those of other companies.

Let's add an additional twist to the helping hand topic.

We are already witnessing the gradual replacement of labor by using robots. Assembly lines and manufacturing plants have continued to adapt robots, oftentimes displacing the labor that previously performed the processing in those facilities.

Here's an intriguing question: *Could a robot be used within a driverless car to provide a helping hand to human passengers?*

A robot as a helping hand is sometimes referred to as a cobot, a newer term that is an amalgamation of the word collaborative and the word robot. These collaborative robots are purposely designed and built to work hand-in-hand with humans. Since we are all familiar with the word robot, more so than the word cobot, herein the word robot will be used, but consider these robots to be akin to cobots.

Furthermore, the robot is not driving the car.

It is essential to realize that this would be a non-driving robot. The robot is in the driverless car to aid human passengers and has no role in driving the car, other than the tangential aspect that the robot would be electronically communicating with the AI that is driving the car.

Let's unpack the matter.

The Levels Of Self-Driving Cars

It is important to clarify what I mean when referring to true self-driving cars.

True self-driving cars are ones that the AI drives the car entirely on its own and there isn't any human assistance during the driving task.

These driverless cars are considered a Level 4 and Level 5, while a car that requires a human driver to co-share the driving effort is usually considered at a Level 2 or Level 3. The cars that co-share the driving task are described as being semi-autonomous, and typically contain a variety of automated add-ons that are referred to as ADAS (Advanced Driver-Assistance Systems).

There is not yet a true self-driving car at Level 5, which we don't yet even know if this will be possible to achieve, and nor how long it will take to get there.

Meanwhile, the Level 4 efforts are gradually trying to get some traction by undergoing very narrow and selective public roadway trials, though there is controversy over whether this testing should be allowed per se (we are all life-or-death guinea pigs in an experiment taking place on our highways and byways, some point out).

Since semi-autonomous cars require a human driver, it would be relatively unlikely that a helping hand robot would be used for such cars. Like every day conventional cars, there's a human driver in the Level 2 and Level 3 car and therefore presumably the human driver would be the helping hand.

It is notable to point out that in spite of those human drivers that keep posting videos of themselves falling asleep at the wheel of a Level 2 or Level 3 car, do not be misled into believing that you can take away your attention from the driving task while driving a semi-autonomous car.

You are the responsible party for the driving actions of the car, regardless of how much automation might be tossed into a Level 2 or Level 3.

Self-Driving Cars And Helping Hand Robots

For Level 4 and Level 5 true self-driving cars, it might be prudent to consider the adoption of helping hand robots.

First, for those that find it exasperating that a robot might already be targeting to replace human labor in the new role of a driverless car nanny or concierge, a role that hasn't even appeared as yet, please realize that there is likely to be a choice available.

When requesting a ridesharing driverless car, the passenger could select either a human helping hand to be provided or indicate that a robot helping hand would be suitable.

It is unlikely that the robot helping hand would be as fully capable as a human helping hand.

Over time, robot technology will gradually improve, eventually becoming more human-like, but in the near-term, the robots being used would be quite limited in comparison to human assistance.

What might these helping hand robots do?

They could physically help while a human is getting into a car. The robot might be within the car and reach out to aid as a passenger gets into the vehicle. Or, the robot might get out of the car and aid as a human gets into the car, and then the robot would get back into the car.

One drawback of any helping hand assistance, whether a human or a robot, involves the aspect that the helper presumably needs to be ultimately seated inside the self-driving car, meaning that some amount of interior space will be taken up by the helper.

Though it's true that the helper would consume interior space, the interior of driverless cars will be more open than a conventional car since there is no longer a set of driving controls that normally take up space.

It is also conceivable that a robot helping hand might fit into the trunk of a car, in which case the robot no longer would necessarily consume interior space. The robot might come out of the trunk to perform its helping duties and then get back into the trunk during a driving journey.

Besides helping humans to get into a car, the helping hand robot could aid as a passenger gets out of the car.

And, the helping hand robot could assist during a driving journey.

It certainly would seem eerie to most of us to see a robot that's seated in a car or that gets out of a car to help a human passenger.

Undoubtedly, a significant cultural change would be needed to accept the notion of such helping hand robots.

In addition, today's robotic technology would be relatively insufficient for this task. The cost of such robots would likely be prohibitive for use in these helping hand tasks. The fluidity of the movement of the robots would be potentially jarring to humans and off-putting. Etc.

Overall, substantial advances in robotics would be needed to make helping hand robots a practical possibility.

If such robots are developed, the odds are that those specialized kinds of robots would be put to other allied uses.

People might have their own at-home robot that serves as a helping hand around the house. Your helping hand robot might be as familiar to you as the Roomba that you use today to clean your floors. A robot around the house could eventually become commonplace.

In which case, a person that uses a driverless car might take along their own helping hand robot and might not need to have one provided by a ridesharing service.

Conclusion

How safe would a helping hand robot be?

That's a good question.

One concern about using a helping hand robot would be whether the robot might inadvertently cause harm.

Suppose the robot accidentally shoved a passenger while trying to aid the person or swung around and bopped someone on their head.

Such robots would need to contain a raft of sensors to detect their surroundings and be programmed to work as safely as possible. Fail-safe capabilities would need to be included. If a helping hand robot turned out to be a harming hand, it would be counterproductive and likely sink the possibility of adopting those kinds of robots (rightfully so, until they are ready for prime-time use).

There is already tremendous interest and progress in developing robots that would deliver packages from a vehicle to the front door of a home.

The so-called "last mile" problem of getting a shipped item out of a car or van and then to the recipient is aiming to be solved by walking or rolling robots. The robot would either place the shipped package at the door or might even hand the package to a human that opens the door.

Most of the major shippers and freight hauling companies are pursuing efforts toward developing or adopting these last-mile robots.

In that sense, we might become used to seeing robots that do package deliveries, and it would seem not a huge leap to then accept that such robots could be a driverless car helping hand.

One step leads to the other.

Might we one day have favored helping hand robots, causing you to request robot Jane or robot Jim, ones that you found to be especially helpful to you?

Yes, it's a real possibility, though do keep in mind that this won't be happening right away and probably our children or our children's children will be the generation that gets to use those helping hand robots.

That day should be marked on our future calendars.

CHAPTER 3
HEALTHTECH
AND
AI SELF-DRIVING CARS

CHAPTER 3

HEALTHTECH
AND
AI SELF-DRIVING CARS

Having to visit the doctor can be arduous.

For those that don't have a car, they oftentimes need to utilize multiple mass transit options and the journey itself is so exasperating and enough of a barrier that they might forego making the visit.

When people don't get over to see a physician, the odds are that whatever prompted them initially to consider going will get worse, ultimately meaning that at some point they will be forced into a visit and the effort and cost to deal with the issue will be heightened.

There's a micro and macro consequence to this:

- *Micro.* In the individual case, this can mean that people suffer while unable to find a means to get to a medical expert and their aliment can progress beyond the point of using simpler methods to solve their health problem.

- *Macro.* In the aggregate, this means that as a society we are inadvertently increasing our costs of healthcare since we aren't catching health issues early and thus having to pony up more medical care and more expensive medical care once the health issue finally starts to get resolved.

Even those that do have a car aren't necessarily on easy street about going to see a medical specialist.

If your ailment is bad enough that you aren't able to safely drive, you need to find someone else to drive your car. The driver would need to be licensed to drive and has to be available to give you a lift, plus they would presumably need to stick around during your appointment so that they could drive you back home.

Today's era of healthcare has tried to acknowledge these downsides by pushing medical assistance further out into where we live and work, rather than always having to go to a centralized place to get care.

For clarity, I somewhat have a dog in this hunt as a former top tech executive at one of the major home healthcare companies, since I firmly believe that the ongoing emergence of having healthcare providers that come out to the home or office has been an exciting and heartening trend, enabling many in society to more readily and easily receive healthcare.

Nicely too, various pharmacies and retail stores now offer an on-site nurse for undertaking a select set of outpatient activities, plus retail brick-and-mortar sites have tried other innovative approaches such as setting up electronic kiosks that provide TV-screen remote access to a wide range of clinicians.

These baby steps in bringing healthcare to people versus people having to get to healthcare are going to be increasingly sought.

Suppose we could wave a magic wand and have healthcare that's available anytime and anyplace?

This brings up an interesting point: *The advent of true self-driving cars and the use of AI HealthTech portends an upcoming surge in any time anyplace healthcare, and many believe it will be an incredible boon to American health and wellness.*

Let's unpack the matter.

The Levels Of Self-Driving Cars

It is important to clarify what I mean when referring to true self-driving cars.

True self-driving cars are ones that the AI drives the car entirely on its own and there isn't any human assistance during the driving task.

These driverless vehicles are considered a Level 4 and Level 5, while a car that requires a human driver to co-share the driving effort is usually considered at a Level 2 or Level 3. The cars that co-share the driving task are described as being semi-autonomous, and typically contain a variety of automated add-on's that are referred to as ADAS (Advanced Driver-Assistance Systems).

There is not yet a true self-driving car at Level 5, which we don't yet even know if this will be possible to achieve, and nor how long it will take to get there.

Meanwhile, the Level 4 efforts are gradually trying to get some traction by undergoing very narrow and selective public roadway trials, though there is controversy over whether this testing should be allowed per se (we are all life-or-death guinea pigs in an experiment taking place on our highways and byways, some point out).

Since semi-autonomous cars require a human driver, the adoption of those types of cars won't be markedly different than driving conventional vehicles, so there's not much new per se to cover about them on this topic (though, as you'll see in a moment, the points next made are generally applicable).

For semi-autonomous cars, it is important that the public be forewarned about a disturbing aspect that's been arising lately, namely that in spite of those human drivers that keep posting videos of themselves falling asleep at the wheel of a Level 2 or Level 3 car, we all need to avoid being misled into believing that the driver can take away their attention from the driving task while driving a semi-autonomous car.

You are the responsible party for the driving actions of the vehicle, regardless of how much automation might be tossed into a Level 2 or Level 3.

Self-Driving Cars Key Elements

For Level 4 and Level 5 true self-driving vehicles, there won't be a human driver involved in the driving task.

All occupants will be passengers.

The AI is doing the driving.

Your first thought might be that this doesn't seem to make any remarkable difference to the matter of getting people-to-healthcare or healthcare-to-people.

Isn't having the AI doing the driving just the same as if you had a human doing the driving, in terms of this question about people and healthcare access?

Actually, it's going to be a sea change.

First, by having the AI do the driving there is no longer the logistics difficulties of finding and using a driver.

The AI is always there in the self-driving car and ready to drive.

No need for coffee breaks. No naps. No limits to perhaps driving just an 8-hour shift and then calling it quits for the day.

In the case of human-driven cars, you need to find someone that is able to drive, presumably properly licensed to drive, and available to drive. There is a likely cost involved in both finding the driver and having them do the driving. Furthermore, while you are seeing a medical specialist, the driver might need to stick around and therefore chew-up more cost as they idly wait for you to finish.

We already have seen that today's ridesharing has helped somewhat to contend with the driving conundrum, but there are still barriers involved. Having a human driver still entails added cost and complexities.

In short, AI-driven self-driving cars are going to make access and use to a car become much easier, presumably at a lower cost, and many pundits have declared that we are heading into a mobility-based economy and a mobility bonanza.

This mobility-for-all will hopefully extend too to those that are today mobility disadvantaged, which in turn suggests that the healthcare needs of those without mobility access are going to be turned around and get a better shot at access to healthcare.

Secondly, by removing a human driver from the driving act, you can free-up the interior of the self-driving car and reshape what the inside of the car has and can do.

Imagine that you no longer were constrained by needing to design a car to have a fixed position at the front seat to encompass a steering wheel and driving pedals.

Automakers are envisioning that the interior of driverless cars will have perhaps swiveling seats, allowing passengers to face each other and carry on conversations, rather than having to awkwardly twist and turn by looking over the seats rooted inside existing conventional cars.

The seats will also fully recline, allowing riders to get some sleep while commuting to work.

The windows of the driverless car are going to be outfitted with LED displays facing inward.

Besides allowing you to use 5G and rapidly stream your favorite Netflix shows, you can also invoke a Facetime-like interactive video chat feature, allowing you to dialogue in real-time with your kids at home while you are stuck in traffic after leaving work.

Let's combine together the aspect that the AI is doing the driving, plus driverless cars will have ready and rapid internet access and the aspect that self-driving cars will have reconstituted interiors.

Turns out to be a potent combination.

New Soup For The Soul

I'll rattle off the myriad of ways that healthcare and people are going to interconnect in a manner that is either new or at least more readily enabled as a result of true self-driving cars:

- **BYOT Wearable HealthTech.** People will likely have their own wearable HealthTech of one kind or another, such as a fitness wristband or a watch that keeps track of their body status and will get into a driverless car wearing their BYOT (Bring Your Own Tech). The AI of the self-driving car will be able to connect with the wearable stuff via API's (well, it will be hodge-podge at first), and thus your car and your health status will be at one during a driving journey (though privacy concerns can arise). For more about how the Internet of Things (IoT) and driverless cars will interplay, see **this link here**.

- **In-Car Wearable HealthTech.** Within self-driving cars, they can come equipped with wearable HealthTech at-the-ready (no need to bring your own), allowing you to get plugged in during a driving journey. You'll easily get your blood pressure reading and other vital health stats, using the provided devices.

- **In-Car AI Healthcare Analyses.** The primary AI of the driverless car is there to drive the car, but this doesn't mean that there can't be other AI modules on-board too. Via the wearables data that are being collected as you travel inside a self-driving car, the AI medical specialty capability can be doing a diagnosis and offer advice about how to enhance your health and wellness.

- **Cloud-Based AI Healthcare Analyses.** The AI that's doing the healthcare stuff doesn't have to be on-board the driverless car and could instead be cloud-based. There's going to be plenty of high-speed internet access inside driverless cars and with the LED displays inside the vehicle, you can pull-up the best AI "specialists" that are versed in specific domains.

- **AI Facial Recognition For Health Status.** Most driverless cars will have cameras that point inward, doing so to allow you to do interactive remote Skype-like sessions while traveling inside the self-driving car. Those cameras can also be used by AI that is able to do facial recognition in a manner that is beyond simply detecting who you are. The latest aspects include detecting your mood or sentiment and possibly uncovering telltale signs of possibly health-related issues via reading your face.

- **AI Voice Recognition For Health Status.** Similar to using AI facial recognition, the AI voice recognition can try to ascertain your health status via how your voice sounds. Thus, rather than only doing voice recognition to figure out what commands or instructions you are giving to the AI system, the AI can attempt to discover telltale signs of potential health-related issues via your voice, such as your having slurred speech or might be experiencing difficulty in forming words and being coherent.

- **Added In-Car Sensors For Health Detection.** Besides the inward-facing cameras, there could be other sensors that are also aimed at the passengers and is used to ascertain health status (such as thermal imaging, etc. of a non-wearable nature). These would be in addition to or in lieu of using wearable HealthTech devices inside the driverless car.

- **Remote Access Combined With AI.** Imagine that you bring up a live session with your doctor, doing so while inside the self-driving car, and meanwhile, the AI elements of the driverless car that pertain to health are also participating. The doctor asks what your temperature is, and the AI quickly jumps in and indicates that via the wearables or via the other sensors it has been tracking your temperature and it has been steadily rising in the twenty minutes you've been riding. The overall notion is that you might interact with human medical specialists and do so in combination with the AI and the HealthTech devices during a driverless car journey.

- **Taking You To Healthcare.** The self-driving car might be taking you to a healthcare provider as per your request to do so, and thus the driverless car is merely a form of transport and not employing other on-board or accessible HealthTech. Meanwhile, the AI might at least be able to reassure you, telling you that you are on your way and you will be getting there soon.

- **Midstream Taking You To Healthcare.** Similar to the aforementioned aspect of taking you to healthcare, this variant consists of you not having initially requested to visit healthcare, but during the driving journey, something has arisen that leads to you needing to do so. The AI might have detected something amiss in your wellness status and then offered to rush you to the nearest healthcare location, or you might have decided that you abruptly need to head to healthcare and have told the AI to aim to a new destination accordingly.

- **Failsafe Option Of Healthcare Destination.** Yet another variant of the process of visiting healthcare is the possibility that someone inside a self-driving car might suddenly collapse and no longer be conscious. If you had a human driver, the odds are that the human driver would realize things are amiss and divert to the nearest emergency room. The AI of the self-driving car can be doing the same kind of monitoring and if the rider seemingly is unresponsive, there could be a "failsafe" option of the driverless car automatically routing to an ER.

- **Rendezvous With Healthcare.** Perhaps the nearest ER or other medical facility is relatively far away. Via the use of V2V (vehicle-to-vehicle) electronic communications, your driverless car could beam out a broadcast asking if there are any other nearby vehicles that contain medical specialists that could help you. The AI of your driverless car then could coordinate a rendezvous with some other self-driving car that has someone capable to help, meeting at the nearest roadway stop. The same kind of rendezvous could be done with ambulances, police, fire trucks, and other authorities that might be able to provide the soonest possible health assistance.

- **Healthcare Provider As A Ride-A-Long.** Some driverless car services might provide an added option of having a human clinician come along in the self-driving car with you. These nurses and other medical specialists might end-up all day long riding in driverless cars, and be available for those that request a self-driving car ridesharing ride and specify that they wish to have a healthcare specialist included for the driving journey (these mobile clinicians and other new job roles will gradually emerge due to the advent of self-driving cars, see **this link here**). You might get your annual flu shot this way.

- **Healthcare Specialty Self-Driving Cars.** Besides the use of everyday "normal" driverless cars, we can expect that healthcare providers are going to purposely outfit fleets of self-driving cars for the purposes of providing on-the-road healthcare access. They'll either buy a bunch of driverless cars or cut a deal with some firm that owns a fleet and agree to jointly turn some of those self-driving cars into a set of rolling healthcare mobile facilities.

- **Transaction-Based Healthcare.** Whatever kind of healthcare activity occurs while riding in a driverless car, in some cases it would be transitory and only be associated with the particular driving journey of that moment, essentially being considered transaction-based.

- **Enduring Based Healthcare.** Unlike the one-time transaction-based healthcare experience of being inside a driverless car, it could be that when you get into the self-driving car it is able to bring up your entire health history. This health history might include all other driverless car trips you've been on, including the health measurements made and analyses done, and might go further and have access to your complete EMR/EHR (Electronic Medical Records or Electronic Health Records) database. Of course, this raises a lot of HIPAA related complications to be figured out.

As you can see, there are numerous emerging possibilities and many more to come.

Conclusion

This all seems nifty, but who's going to pay for it?

Lots of options already exist and will be developed:

- People that opt to use self-driving cars might be presented with various optional fees for using an AI HealthTech savvy driverless car and be able to decide whether they want to incur those added fees or not.

- Automakers and other firms that deploy fleets of driverless cars might decide to compete against each other in gaining market share of having people choose to use their brand of self-driving cars, doing so by offering AI HealthTech capabilities as a competitive advantage to lure riders to them.

- Health insurers might encourage people to use AI HealthTech aware self-driving cars, doing so if they believe that it will ultimately decrease the cost of healthcare by earlier and more pervasively conducting health and wellness efforts.

- The government might likewise determine that using self-driving cars in this manner is an overall benefit for society, accomplishing in the aggregate expanded access to healthcare, and therefore could be included as valid reimbursements for government underwritten costs of enabling health and wellness care.

- And so on.

At this time, we don't yet have enough self-driving cars at even Level 4 to adequately explore how this new mobility era is going to intertwine with healthcare.

As such, we are only at the beginning cusp of what might come next.

I'll bet you this, some number of years from now, when true self-driving cars and AI are prevalent, they will be so immersed into healthcare aspects that we'll wonder how we ever got along without them being interwoven into a cohesive and comprehensive whole.

You can take that bet to the bank

CHAPTER 4

RUDEST DRIVERS
AND
AI SELF-DRIVING CARS

CHAPTER 4

RUDEST DRIVERS AND
AI SELF-DRIVING CARS

What kind of car do you drive?

I don't mean whether it is a four-door or two-door, nor whether it is red in color or blue.

Specifically, what brand of car do you drive?

According to various studies, supposedly the brand of car is a telltale indicator of how rude a driver sits behind the wheel of the vehicle.

In other words, it is believed that the rudest drivers tend to drive certain brands of cars. That being said, it is perhaps one of those chicken-or-the-egg dilemmas, in the sense that does a rude driver opt to drive a particular brand or does a specific brand of car perchance attract rude drivers? Nobody can say for sure.

Some even go so far as to suggest that a driver becomes "corrupted" into being a rude driver by the simple act of being in the driver's seat of certain brands of cars.

Maybe on an everyday basis, you are the most civil of drivers, and yet magically you transform once you grasp the steering wheel and put your foot on the gas pedal of these adverse-transformational car brands.

Your honor, the car I was driving made me drive fast and furiously (not sure if a judge will let you get away with that excuse).

Which brands seem to provoke this rudeness in driving?

One study of UK drivers listed Audi drivers as the rudest drivers, followed by BMW, Range Rover, Mercedes, VW, and other brands.

Another wider survey found that BMW drivers were perceived as the rudest drivers, followed closely by Ford, Audi, and others.

Yet another study that was based on incidents of alleged reckless driving (per an insurance firm's records), listed brands and specific makes as the Top 10 "most reckless":
1. Mazda MX-5 Miata
2. Hyundai Genesis Coupe
3. Isuzu Rodeo
4. Nissan 370Z
5. Chevrolet K1500
6. Cadillac ATS
7. VW CC
8. RAM 1500
9. Saturn L200
10. Dodge Challenger

I realize that some of you will be quite upset about being stereotyped as a rude driver simply due to the brand of car that you drive.

It's those other idiots driving around that are the dolts, and you are merely reacting to their foolhardy ways of driving.

Or, possibly you are the exception to the rule, namely that you drive a car that normally is one cast as a rudeness driver magnet, but you don't drive that way. You are a kind and courteous driver.

Come to think of it, the entire topic might be faulty.

Suppose that all car drivers are about equal in rudeness, and we are sensitized by the media to perceive that certain car brands attract rude drivers. As such, you might especially note a rude act when it is done by one of those media-tainted brands, while you ignore or discount rudeness when it is done while a driver is in some other nondescript brand.

Of course, the whole topic could seem overly academic since you might wonder what difference it makes anyway.

Drivers will drive as they opt to drive.

Does it matter if specific brands happen to also tend to have rude drivers?

Well, it could.

When teaching a novice teenager how to drive, some parents will offer a cautionary warning to the youthful pupil on being guarded when getting near certain brands of cars. The novice learns that the odds of getting cutoff or having a rude driver ride on their bumper are heightened when certain brands of cars get nearby to them.

Right or wrong, this does appear to be a helpful rule-of-thumb.

Here's today's intriguing question: *Should AI-based true self-driving cars be aware of which brands tend to have rude human-drivers, and if so, will it be a help or hindrance to self-driving actions?*

Let's unpack the matter and see.

The Levels Of Self-Driving Cars

It is important to clarify what I mean when referring to true self-driving cars.

True self-driving cars are ones that the AI drives the car entirely on its own and there isn't any human assistance during the driving task.

These driverless vehicles are considered a Level 4 and Level 5, while a car that requires a human driver to co-share the driving effort is usually considered at a Level 2 or Level 3. The cars that co-share the driving task are described as being semi-autonomous, and typically contain a variety of automated add-on's that are referred to as ADAS (Advanced Driver-Assistance Systems).

There is not yet a true self-driving car at Level 5, which we don't yet even know if this will be possible to achieve, and nor how long it will take to get there.

Meanwhile, the Level 4 efforts are gradually trying to get some traction by undergoing very narrow and selective public roadway trials, though there is controversy over whether this testing should be allowed per se (we are all life-or-death guinea pigs in an experiment taking place on our highways and byways, some point out).

Since semi-autonomous cars require a human driver, the adoption of those types of cars won't be markedly different than driving conventional vehicles, so there's not much new per se to cover about them on this topic (though, as you'll see in a moment, the points next made are generally applicable).

For semi-autonomous cars, it is important that the public be forewarned about a disturbing aspect that's been arising lately, namely that in spite of those human drivers that keep posting videos of themselves falling asleep at the wheel of a Level 2 or Level 3 car, we all need to avoid being misled into believing that the driver can take away their attention from the driving task while driving a semi-autonomous car.

You are the responsible party for the driving actions of the vehicle, regardless of how much automation might be tossed into a Level 2 or Level 3.

Self-Driving Cars And Rude Drivers

For Level 4 and Level 5 true self-driving vehicles, there won't be a human driver involved in the driving task.

All occupants will be passengers.

The AI is doing the driving.

First, let's tackle a question that some assume is already resolved, but for which it actually remains somewhat open.

Will AI-based true self-driving cars be rude drivers?

Your initial reaction would be that there should never be a cause for a driverless car to act rudely. Thus, without any doubt, there will never be a rude self-driving car, you so assume.

Not so sure about that.

Start with the reaction that some human drivers are having to today's self-driving car tryouts on our public roads.

In most cases, the driverless cars are moving at the posted speed limit, or less so, and driving in an extremely cautionary manner.

As a result, human drivers that encounter self-driving cars are at times getting frustrated and upset at this kind of timidity in driving. Those human drivers will sometimes scoot around the driverless car, dangerously so, and on other occasions will show their displeasure by getting in front of the plodding self-driving car and tap on their brakes to make the driverless car react.

Who is being rude in these circumstances?

You might say that human drivers are being rude.

On the other hand, those alleged "rude" drivers say they are frustrated by the driverless car stiltedness and would claim that the self-driving car is being rude.

The rudeness of the AI-based driving actions is intolerable and a hazard to traffic, they would contend, and though their own rudeness in the reaction is perhaps not laudable, it is solely based on the rudeness of the driverless car to begin with.

Do you buy into that logic?

Some do, many do not.

Anyway, there are pundits that argue that rudeness is simply in the eye of the beholder.

Yet another factor about the potential rudeness of self-driving cars involves our everyday driving practices as humans.

Humans nudge toward other cars to showcase that they want to merge into their lane.

Is this an act of rudeness or an act of subtly indicating your upcoming driving action to other drivers?

If we want self-driving cars to drive similarly to how humans drive, presumably the AI-based driving systems should likewise use the nudging technique for getting into another lane. Without a mimicking action, human drivers might be at a loss for understanding what the driverless car is trying to do.

As such, it could be that we would actively want self-driving cars to be "rude" to the degree that human drivers perform telling micro-maneuvers as they drive.

Though, at some point, there might be a rudeness spectrum level upon which we don't want a self-driving car to end-up. In essence, maybe a little bit of rudeness is fine, but once the rudeness rises above a certain threshold, it's gotten out-of-hand.

Who will decide what the rudeness threshold ought to be?

Should it be the maker of the driverless car, or owner of the self-driving car, or the passengers, or a governmental agency, or whom?

The answer is complicated too by the cultural driving practices of each locale.

Human drivers in New York City are known for being extremely aggressive. In theory, the rudeness factor of a driverless car that's driving in NYC could be a lot higher than if that self-driving car was driving in say hometown Iowa.

Perhaps the AI system should automatically recalibrate its rudeness levels for wherever it might be driving at the time.

Indeed, via OTA (Over-The-Air) electronic updating of the onboard AI system, some suggest that driverless cars will load-in a specialized driving template depending upon the locale being driven. A self-driving car that you use to drive across the United States might end-up loading various driving preferences and parameters that are suitable to the myriad of towns and cities that the driving journey traverses.

Even the time of day and day of the week could make a difference.

In Los Angeles traffic, the morning commute and late afternoon commutes tend to involve lots of rudeness encounters during the weekdays. Late at night, the rudeness often is not as extensive, and somewhat the same on the weekends.

Presumably, the volume of traffic and the urgency of the drivers are instrumental to the rudeness expressions, all of which can vary depending upon the time of day, day of the week, and likely time of the year.

In short, since we are going to have a mixture of human-driven cars and a gradually rising number of self-driving cars, it will be a mixture that inexorably is going to encompass rudeness, likely for many decades to come.

Those that hope for a world in which there are only self-driving cars on the roadways are going to have to hold their breaths for a long time, and indeed it might never be the case that we have only driverless cars (well, today, there are some that say they will cling to being able to drive and you'll only get them out by prying their dead cold hands from the steering wheel).

If the far future does consist of exclusively having driverless cars on our roadways, yes, they could all be civil toward each other and perhaps we could abandon or obliterate any rudeness in driving, though that day is a starry-eyed dream right now.

Ascertaining the Potential For Rudeness

The preceding jaunt covered the aspects of having driverless cars that might or might not exhibit rudeness in driving.

There's another angle to the topic.

An important element to driving involves being able to anticipate the driving actions of others.

Each time that you get behind the wheel, you begin immediately to watch the traffic scene and try to predict what might happen around you.

Will that pedestrian standing at the curb opt to suddenly step into the street in front of your car?

Will the driver ahead of you decide to surprisingly hit their brakes rather than gradually slowing down?

And so on.

Human drivers' size-up the driving situation and make decisions about their own driving accordingly.

Do you glance at other cars and note the brands of cars?

If so, perhaps you are doing so to anticipate that certain brands of cars are most likely being driven by rude drivers, and therefore you need to be on top of your game for a sudden rude action by those drivers.

It can be a crucial split-second difference between being ready for what another driver might do.

Let's return to the topic of driverless cars and consider how we want the AI-based driving systems to act.

A driverless car that does not appropriately anticipate the driving actions of human drivers is going to find itself getting into driving troubles. One way or another, the odds are that the self-driving car will at some point in time hit a human-driven car, or a human-driven car will hit the self-driving car.

Some pundits keep saying that we'll never have any car accidents again, once we have driverless cars.

This is just crazy talk.

We are going to have car accidents that involve self-driving cars and human-driven cars, and as I've already mentioned, the mixing of driverless cars on our roadways and human-driven cars is going to occur for a long time to come.

I might also add that even if we someday have only self-driving cars on the roadways, there are still opportunities for car accidents to occur, such as a pedestrian that darts into the street in front of a self-driving car, and for which the physics of the moment belies the chances of the driverless car stopping in time (we hopefully will have much fewer car accidents, but it decidedly won't become zero, a nice goal but unachievable per se).

Overall, the key point is that we would certainly want self-driving cars to be able to anticipate the actions of other cars, especially human-driven cars.

Statistically, if it were true that certain brands of cars that are being driven by humans were more likely to drive in a rude and abrupt manner, we would likely want to have the driverless cars be aware of this predilection.

As such, the AI-based system could be on its toes, so to speak, ready to cope with an otherwise unexpected driving action by those drivers.

For those that drive those brands of cars, you might be disturbed to think that the AI is sizing up your driving by the mere act of detecting the brand or make/model of the car you are driving.

But, humans seem to do so, and thus why not have the self-driving car do likewise?

Some might say that if the shoe fits, so be it, since you chose the shoe you are wearing.

Others are worried that the AI system is unfairly categorizing other drivers, doing so not by their overt actions, and instead merely by the type of car.

And, it could be a slippery slope, namely that driverless cars would use other criteria, perhaps racially-biased, or gender-based, or age-based, and begin anticipating driving behaviors on a discriminatory basis.

Conclusion

Believe it or not, some drivers that do drive the "rudeness brands" are proud to do so.

They relish that other drivers believe them to be rude drivers.

In fact, their viewpoint is that if other drivers stay out of their way, solely as a result of the brand of a car being driven, it is a blessing and they are happy to derive the benefits thereof.

This adds yet another twist to the self-driving car topic.

Suppose that self-driving cars are more apt to give driving advantages to "rude" categorized human-driven cars, allowing those cars to more readily cut into a lane or make that upcoming left turn.

Wouldn't the rudeness categorization be rewarding those that happen to buy or use a car that fits within the alleged rudeness driving brands?

People that figured out that the AI was doing this might be tempted to purposely buy or rent a "rudeness" brand of car, figuring they would then be able to speed along and get away with annoying driving behavior, at least as far as the self-driving cars on the roadways were concerned.

Backing up for a moment on the topic, another facet that needs to be considered involves the use of Machine Learning (ML) and Deep Learning (DL) as it relates to driving behaviors.

Many of the automakers and self-driving tech firms are collecting vast amounts of traffic driving data to use for AI ML/DL to figure out how to best drive on our roads (identifying patterns in how we drive).

In theory, if we as humans are currently driving in a manner that lets rude drivers get away with rude driving, presumably any collected traffic-driving data would silently have such patterns contained within it.

The AI ML/DL might pick-up on those patterns, and then guide the AI driving systems accordingly, meaning that they would inherently be anticipating rude driving behavior, and might well do so on the basis of car brands (if that's an identified factor during the ML/DL mathematical computations).

Yikes!

In that case, perhaps we might want to declare that simply because things have been done that way (in terms of societal acceptance of rude driving), it does not mean they should be continued or further promulgated in that way.

Would we want the emerging crop of self-driving cars to set a new tone and try to reduce or undercut the prevalence of human-driven rudeness in driving?

For those of you that say yes, of course, keep in mind that some argue that once we start to use self-driving cars to shape human driving behavior, perhaps it is a stepping stone toward having AI guide overall human behavior, and on that slippery slope we might ultimately all end-up as slaves of AI.

And to think it all started by the mere act of trying to cope with rude drivers.

CHAPTER 5
ALIENS ON EARTH
AND
AI SELF-DRIVING CARS

CHAPTER 5
ALIENS ON EARTH
AND
AI SELF-DRIVING CARS

Stay with me on this one.

According to a news report, Britain's first astronaut has indicated that there could be alien beings living among us on Earth: "It's possible they're here right now and we simply can't see them."

Furthermore, an equally remarkable assertion was made: "Aliens exist, there's no two ways about it."

That astronaut, Helen Patricia Sharman, had gone on a space mission in May of 1991, doing so to visit the Soviet Mir space station, and famously was the first of seven British astronauts that ultimately have ventured into outer space.

Despite the seemingly incredulous idea of aliens residing here right now, step back for a moment and consider whether she might know something that the rest of us do not.

Could she have seen something or experienced something while in outer space that has given her a heightened sensitivity to detecting otherworldly phenomena?

Maybe cosmic rays soaked her body and mind, producing or stoking a dormant cognitive capability that allows for sensing the presence of alien species. Similar to how your pet dog or cat has a kind of sixth sense that we humans do not have; it could be that Helen now possesses a subliminal capability of sensing strange visitors to our planet.

Admittedly, realizing that there have been over 550 people that have gone into outer space, one must ask how come the other space travelers have not had the same revelation.

Come to think of it, maybe some have indeed experienced the same, but are tightlipped else concerned that the rest of us Earth bounded populous might misperceive them as crazy or mentally unhinged.

Put yourself into their shoes.

If you suspected that there were alien creatures here, yet you had no solid proof and merely had a nagging inner feeling about it, would you speak up?

On the one hand, perhaps as a loyal human to humanity, you might feel it was your duty to let the rest of us know what's happening.

But, since there's seemingly no means to validate your claim, would you be merely ridiculed, and anyway what good would it do if humanity actually acknowledged that aliens were nestled here on Earth.

Okay, go with that last thought.

Let's momentarily agree that there are aliens from outer space right here, right now, and while you are reading this sentence, they could be near you, looking over your shoulder, or possibly far away on another continent.

Perhaps they are here in human form.

If so, do we have any tangible means to ascertain that a human walking past you is a real human or instead an alien creature?

There are no such means today, though maybe top-secret scientists have come up with a way to do so and the device or mechanism is securely locked-up in Area 51.

Rather than taking on human form, those sneaky aliens could be disguised as dogs, or cats, or some other kind of animal.

It's not clear why the aliens would find it advantageous to be in the form of an animal. Yes, they could readily roam around Earth and fit in, though they are restricted in a myriad of ways, else we humans would get suspicious.

Perhaps their physical form constrains them to be shaped only into animals, or perhaps they are able to take over the bodies of animals and cannot do the same with humans (humans might be uninhabitable, or our minds might be impervious to alien occupation, meanwhile animals are their easiest target).

The aliens might be microorganisms.

As such, they are so tiny that they could be just about anywhere.

Another possibility is that the aliens are immersed in another dimension, one that we cannot see or enter into.

The British astronaut might have somehow miraculously become attached to a mini-portal into that other dimension, or there was leakage from the unseen dimension that happened while she was circling the Earth in outer space.

One wonders, why haven't the aliens shown themselves to us?

In other words, if they are here, and we don't know it, they are essentially hiding, at least to the degree that we don't know they are here.

When I say the word "hiding" it could be that they are in plain sight and they don't believe themselves to be hiding, but the reality is that if we aren't able to see them or have discourse with them, in a manner of speaking they are in fact hiding.

With that logic, we need to consider that they are hiding because they have no means to show themselves to us, or they are hiding because they are waiting for something to trigger them to come out of hiding.

The trigger might suddenly allow them to interact with us, which otherwise they've not been able to do so.

Or, the trigger might alert them that it is finally time to interact with us.

Most doomsday stories about such matters involve the aliens then killing off humans and opting to take over Earth, or as a minimum, turning humans into slaves of one kind or another.

Since we've come this far into the speculation rabbit hole, the next consideration would naturally be about the trigger.

What is the trigger?

A common favorite is that humans find themselves hazardously entering into a global catastrophic war and this somehow triggers the aliens to shift into action.

I'd like to think that maybe the aliens are waiting instead for humanity to utterly dispense with war and fighting altogether, and the trigger is invoked once humans' band together in total peace and harmony, upon which the aliens then show themselves.

Of course, the problem there is that the chances of humanity embracing a purity of soul is seemingly improbable (sorry, that's the glass is a half-empty viewpoint, I realize), and thus it means that those aliens are going to have a long, long, long wait (forever?).

Anyway, what other type of trigger might be the spark?

Here's an intriguing question for you: *Could the advent of AI-based true self-driving cars be the long-awaited trigger that causes the hidden alien beings to suddenly show themselves here on Earth?*

Conceding that this whole saga is rather outlandish speculation, to begin with, the notion that somehow AI-based self-driving cars are involved might appear to be highly speculative, but there's an old saying that if the premise is outlandish you can ergo proceed into a conclusion that's equally outlandish.

Let's unpack the matter and see.

The Levels Of Self-Driving Cars

It is important to clarify what I mean when referring to AI-based true self-driving cars.

True self-driving cars are ones that the AI drives the car entirely on its own and there isn't any human assistance during the driving task.

These driverless vehicles are considered a Level 4 and Level 5, while a car that requires a human driver to co-share the driving effort is usually considered at a Level 2 or Level 3. The cars that co-share the driving task are described as being semi-autonomous, and typically contain a variety of automated add-on's that are referred to as ADAS (Advanced Driver-Assistance Systems).

There is not yet a true self-driving car at Level 5, which we don't yet even know if this will be possible to achieve, and nor how long it will take to get there.

Meanwhile, the Level 4 efforts are gradually trying to get some traction by undergoing very narrow and selective public roadway trials, though there is controversy over whether this testing should be allowed per se (we are all life-or-death guinea pigs in an experiment taking place on our highways and byways, some point out).

Since semi-autonomous cars require a human driver, the adoption of those types of cars won't be markedly different than driving conventional vehicles, so there's not much new per se to cover about them on this topic (though, as you'll see in a moment, the points next made are generally applicable).

For semi-autonomous cars, it is important that the public be forewarned about a disturbing aspect that's been arising lately, namely that in spite of those human drivers that keep posting videos of themselves falling asleep at the wheel of a Level 2 or Level 3 car, we all need to avoid being misled into believing that the driver can take away their attention from the driving task while driving a semi-autonomous car.

You are the responsible party for the driving actions of the vehicle, regardless of how much automation might be tossed into a Level 2 or Level 3.

Self-Driving Cars And Triggering Those Beings

For Level 4 and Level 5 true self-driving vehicles, there won't be a human driver involved in the driving task.

All occupants will be passengers.

The AI is doing the driving.

Most pundits would agree that the advent of true self-driving cars is going to help humanity, allowing for access to mobility that today is overly limited. Those that are mobility disadvantaged will find themselves finally able to get around.

In addition, it is anticipated that the number of lives saved is going to be another tremendous benefit of true self-driving cars.

Today, in the United States alone, there are about 40,000 deaths per year due to car crashes and another 2.3 million estimated injuries. It is hoped that by-and-large there won't be many car crashes anymore and therefore those deaths and injuries will be pretty much averted (though, please know, I have some heartburn about the misleading claims of achieving zero fatalities).

Seems like a rosy future ahead.

Might the emergence of AI self-driving cars somehow be the trigger for those hidden aliens to show themselves?

At first glance, there doesn't seem to be any apparent reason that the advent of AI-based true self-driving cars could or should be the extraordinary trigger.

Don't despair, sometimes the inapparent can be made into the apparent.

Here are three notable reasons, each having their own separate merit as a trigger inducing basis.

Strap yourself in.

1. *A Ready Form of Transport*

Keep in mind that today's cars require a human driver.

AI-based true self-driving cars do not require a human driver, and it is also generally assumed that there won't be any provision at all for a human driver (in essence, the driving will exclusively be done by the AI system, and no human driving will be permitted, thus the steering wheel and pedals will be ripped out of cars).

We could ultimately have an entire transportation ecosystem based on autonomy.

There might be self-driving cars, self-driving trucks, self-driving buses, self-driving trains, self-driving planes, self-driving drones, self-driving scooters, self-driving motorcycles, and so on.

End-to-end, as you travel, there won't be any human at all involved in terms of driving the vehicle that you are using for your transport.

Perhaps that's what those hidden alien beings are waiting for.

Today, they would require human assistance in being transported.

In the future, they presumably would not need human assistance to be transported.

And, in some sense, humans might be less aware of the aliens traveling among us, during an era of all self-driving vehicles.

How so?

You need to realize that self-driving cars and other such vehicles will likely be roaming around a lot of the time without any human passengers in those vehicles.

For much of the time, it is predicted that self-driving cars will be on the go and continually roaming so as to be available when a human requires a lift.

As I've previously exhorted, this means that we could have some adverse consequences, involving lots of wasted energy consumption by empty self-driving cars going up and down our streets, trolling for a fare. This could also chew-up our roadways, increasing costs to maintain our highways and byways, and it could actually lead to worsened congestion rather than opening up traffic on our roadways.

Setting aside those concerns, the point being that if the aliens are hidden now, they could potentially remain somewhat hidden and yet be able to more readily get around, merely by hitching a ride on roaming self-driving cars.

If you saw a car coming down the street today and it seemed entirely empty, you'd be startled and would certainly take notice.

In the future, if you see a self-driving car that's making its way through downtown on its own, seemingly empty, you won't even give it a glance.

Could there be an alien creature using it to get from point A to point B?

Maybe.

2. *Seeking Control Over Our Mobility*

The preceding reason was relatively benign and did not necessarily suggest that the aliens would use the advent of self-driving cars to dominate or overtake humans.

Time to up the ante.

Once we get to having a transportation ecosystem of purely self-driving capabilities, it means that we all will be fully dependent upon autonomous systems for our mobility.

There is some debate about whether we will have a provision for humans to take the wheel of self-driving vehicles, which many say we should, as a precaution, though others insist that we should not allow humans to drive anymore since it would lamentably open the door (once again) to human foibles while driving (such as distracted driving, drunk driving, and the like).

Get humans entirely out-of-the-loop, some argue.

Okay, under that scenario, and if you are a hiding alien, it would sure seem like a handy time to try and take over humanity.

Assuming that the aliens could take over the AI systems that are doing the driving, those pesky and clever aliens would henceforth control our mobility, entirely, across the globe.

The mobility-for-all mantra gets turned on its head.

Instead, we become trapped by our own devised mobility autonomy and the aliens could easily restrict our movement.

It just shows how humans can sometimes lay the path of their own destruction, though we don't know that the aliens would destroy us per se and perhaps merely imprison us here on Earth.

So that this option doesn't depress you, the smiley face version is that the aliens are benevolent and somehow by controlling our movement prevent us from self-destruction.

That's a stretch.

3. *Mates With AI*

The third reason that the aliens might be triggered via the advent of AI-based true self-driving cars is the AI part of the equation.

If we are able to devise AI systems that are good enough to provide fully self-driving capabilities, some wonder if that means we'll have advanced AI to amazingly high levels of intelligence-like behavior.

Toss aside the mobility part of the formula and focus solely on the AI.

Suppose that we've perfected AI systems to the degree that are nearly "intelligent" and approaching what some denote as the singularity (this is when AI systems crossover into being sentient).

Perhaps the aliens are waiting for us to develop AI that's near to human intelligence, and at that juncture, the aliens are going to mate or infuse themselves with those AI systems.

Until then, the aliens presumably didn't have a means to fully emerge, and they needed to have a "vehicle" to do so (not a car, not a train, not a plane, but instead a massively scaled AI system that's sufficiently capable of intelligent-like performance).

I'll leave it to you to decide whether this provides a foul outcome or a favorable outcome.

The upbeat version is that the aliens are finally able to communicate with us, and we all become one happy family, residing together on Earth in peace and harmony (yes, still aiming for that, thanks).

I won't trouble you with the downbeat version.

Conclusion

What a lot of crazy talk, some of you must be thinking.

There's no doubt that the topic is at the edge of reason.

I would ask that you at least realize that by discussing this topic, it does bring up some important societal aspects about the future of self-driving cars and self-driving vehicles of all kinds, and likewise raises important questions about the future of AI.

Ignore the stuff about alien beings and focus instead on the autonomy elements.

For example:

- Do we want to become wholly dependent on autonomous AI-driven systems, or should we still allow for human driving provisions too?

- Does the AI that will be doing the driving need to be intelligent-like, or can it be a lot less so, though does that mean that we are having self-driving that's stilted and not as overall capable as human driving?

- Could there be facets to the mobility-for-all that aren't as rosy as we might otherwise assume, and thus we should be anticipating those so-called "unanticipated" adverse consequences that might arise?

- If we are able to push AI sufficiently toward the alleged singularity, what might happen once we get there, and should we allow ourselves to reach that point by inertia alone, rather than by explicitly deliberated awareness of what we are achieving or potentially unleashing?

And so on.

None of those worthwhile considerations have anything to do with hidden alien beings per se.

In a sense, the alien beings premise provides the sugar coating for getting us all to take the medicine that we need to put some serious thought into what a self-driving world will be like, along with what a world that has extremely advanced AI will be like.

The good news, one could argue, involves the aspect that we are still a long way away from arriving at true self-driving, and even further away from any widespread adoption of self-driving, allowing us time to discuss and debate these meaty topics.

In terms of AI that's going to achieve singularity, I argue that we are unquestionably a long way from that happening, and thus we have time to figure out whether we want to get there and if so what we will do once we arrive.

Not everyone agrees about the timing of these matters, including some that suggest we are near to achieving self-driving and we are also near to achieving a singularity.

No time to waste then about giving due consideration to these weighty matters.

Shift gears for one last thought.

If there are aliens hiding out here, and if they are able to read, do you think that as they read about our suspicions of alien creatures hidden here on Earth, are they laughing at us because they know we can't see them, or are they shaking in their boots that we might somehow luck out and detect them?

And the next time you see an "empty" self-driving car as shown in a video or going down the street near you, you might find yourself quietly wondering whether it truly is empty or maybe giving a free lift to an earthly being from another planet.

Those freeloading deadbeats.

.

CHAPTER 6
AI HUMAN RIGHTS AND
AI SELF-DRIVING CARS

CHAPTER 6

AI HUMAN RIGHTS AND
AI SELF-DRIVING CARS

Should AI have human rights?

It's a seemingly simple question, though the answer has tremendous consequences.

Presumably, your answer is either that yes, AI should have human rights, or alternatively, that AI should not have human rights.

Take a pick.

But pick wisely.

There is a bit of a trick involved though because the thing or entity or "being" that we are trying to assign human rights to is currently ambiguous and currently not even yet in existence.

In other words, what does it mean when we refer to "AI" and how will we know it when we discover or invent it?

At this time, there isn't any AI system of any kind that could be considered sentient, and indeed by all accounts, we aren't anywhere close to achieving the so-called singularity (that's the point at which AI flips over into becoming sentient and we look in awe at a presumably human-equivalent intelligence embodied in a machine).

I'm not saying that we won't ever reach that vaunted point, yet there are some that fervently argue we won't.

I suppose it's a tossup as to whether getting to the singularity is something to be sought or to be feared.

For those that look at the world in a smiley face way, perhaps AI that is our equivalent in intelligence will aid us in solving up-until-now unsolvable problems, such as aiding in finding a cure for cancer or being able to figure out how to overcome world hunger.

In essence, our newfound buddy will boost our aggregate capacity of intelligence and be an instrumental contributor towards the betterment of humanity.

I'd like to think that's what will happen.

On the other hand, for those of you that are more doom-and-gloom oriented (perhaps rightfully so), you are gravely worried that this AI might decide it would rather be the master versus the slave and could opt on a massive scale to take over humans.

Plus, especially worrisome, the AI might ascertain that humans aren't worthwhile anyway, and off with the heads of humanity.

As a human, I not particularly keen on that outcome.

All in all, the question about AI and human rights is right now a rather theoretical exercise since there isn't this topnotch type of AI yet crafted (of course, it's always best to be ready for a potentially rocky future, thus, discussing the topic beforehand does have merit).

One supposes that we could consider the question of human rights as it might apply to AI that's a lesser level of capability than the (maybe) insurmountable threshold of sentience.

Keep in mind that doing this, lowering the bar, could open a potential Pandoras box of where the bar should be set at.

Here's how.

Imagine that you are trying to do pull-ups and the rule is that you need to get your chin up above the bar.

It becomes rather straightforward to ascertain whether or not you've done an actual pull-up.

If your chin doesn't get over that bar, it's not considered a true pull-up. Furthermore, it doesn't matter whether your chin ended-up a quarter inch below the bar, nor whether it was three inches below the bar. Essentially, you either make it clearly over the bar, or you don't.

In the case of AI, if the "bar" is the achievement of sentience, and if we are willing to allow that some alternative place below the bar will count for having achieved AI, where might we draw that line?

You might argue that if the AI can write poetry, voila, it is considered true AI.

In existing parlance, some refer to this as a form of narrow AI, meaning AI that can do well in a narrow domain, but this does not ergo mean that the AI can do particularly well in any other domains (likely not).

Someone else might say that writing poetry is not sufficient and that instead if AI can figure out how the universe began, the AI would be good enough, and though it isn't presumably fully sentient, it nonetheless is deserving of human rights.

Or, at least deserving of the consideration of being granted human rights (which, maybe humanity won't decide upon until the day after the grand threshold is reached, whatever the threshold is that might be decided upon since we do often like to wait until the last moment to make thorny decisions).

The point being that we might indubitably argue endlessly about how far below the bar that we would collectively agree is the point at which AI has gotten good enough for which it then falls into the realm of possibly being assigned human rights.

For those of you that say that this matter isn't so complicated and you'll certainly know it (i.e., AI), when you see it, there's a famous approach called the Turing Test that seeks to clarify how to figure out whether AI has reached human-like intelligence, but there are lots of twists and turns that make this surprisingly for some a lot more unsure than you might assume.

In short, once we agree that going below the sentience bar is allowed, the whole topic gets really murky and possibly undecidable due to trying to reach consensus on whether a quarter inch below, or three inches below, or several feet below the bar is sufficient.

Wait a second, some are exhorting, why do we need to even consider granting human rights to a machine anyway?

Well, some believe that a machine that showcases human-like intelligence ought to be treated with the same respect that we would give to another human.

A brief tangent herein might be handy to ponder.

You might know that there is an acrimonious and ongoing debate about whether animals should have the same rights as humans.

There are some people that vehemently say yes, while there are others that claim it is absurd to assign human rights to "creatures" that are not able to exhibit the same intelligence as humans do (sure, there are admittedly some might clever animals, but once again if the bar is a form of sentience that is wrapped into the fullest nature of human intelligence, we are back to the issue of how much do we lower the "bar" to accommodate them, in this case accommodating everyday animals).

Some would say that until the day upon which animals are able to write poetry and intellectually contribute to other vital aspects of humanities pursuits, they can have some form of "animal rights" but by-gosh they aren't "qualified" for getting the revered human rights.

Please know that I don't want to take us down the rabbit hole on animal rights, and so let's set that aside for the moment, realizing that I brought it up just to mention that the assignment of human rights is clearly a touchy topic and one that goes beyond the realm of debates about AI.

Okay, I've highlighted herein that the "AI" mentioned in the question of assigning human rights is ambiguous and not even yet achieved.

You might be curious about what it means to refer to "human rights" and whether we can all generally agree to what that consists of.

Fortunately, yes, generally we do have some agreement on that matter.

I'm referring to the United Nations promulgation of the Universal Declaration of Human Rights (UDHR).

Be aware that there are some critics that don't like the UDHR, including those that criticize its wording, some believe it doesn't cover enough rights, some assert that it is vague and misleading, etc.

Look, I'm not saying it is perfect, nor that it is necessarily "right and true," but at least it is a marker or line-in-the-sand, and we can use it for the needed purposes herein.

Namely, for a debate and discussion about assigning human rights to AI, let's allow that this thought experiment on this weighty matter can be undertaken with respect to using the UDHR as a means of expressing what we intend overall as human rights.

In a moment, I'll identify some of the human rights spelled out in the UDHR, and we can explore what might happen if those human rights were assigned to AI.

One other quick remark.

Many assume that AI of a sentience capacity will of necessity be rooted in a robot.

Not necessarily.

There could be a sentient AI that is embodied in something other than a "robot" (most people assume a robot is a machine that has robotic arms, robotic legs, robotic hands, and overall looks like a human being, though a robot can refer to a much wider variety of machine instantiations).

Let's then consider the following idea: *What might happen if we assign human rights to AI and we are all using AI-based true self-driving cars as our only form of transportation?*

Time to unpack the matter and see.

The Levels Of Self-Driving Cars

It is important to clarify what I mean when referring to AI-based true self-driving cars.

True self-driving cars are ones that the AI drives the car entirely on its own and there isn't any human assistance during the driving task.

These driverless vehicles are considered a Level 4 and Level 5, while a car that requires a human driver to co-share the driving effort is usually considered at a Level 2 or Level 3. The cars that co-share the driving task are described as being semi-autonomous, and typically contain a variety of automated add-on's that are referred to as ADAS (Advanced Driver-Assistance Systems).

There is not yet a true self-driving car at Level 5, which we don't yet even know if this will be possible to achieve, and nor how long it will take to get there.

Meanwhile, the Level 4 efforts are gradually trying to get some traction by undergoing very narrow and selective public roadway trials, though there is controversy over whether this testing should be allowed per se (we are all life-or-death guinea pigs in an experiment taking place on our highways and byways, some point out).

Since semi-autonomous cars require a human driver, the adoption of those types of cars won't be markedly different than driving conventional vehicles, so there's not much new per se to cover about them on this topic (though, as you'll see in a moment, the points next made are generally applicable).

For semi-autonomous cars, it is important that the public be forewarned about a disturbing aspect that's been arising lately, namely that in spite of those human drivers that keep posting videos of themselves falling asleep at the wheel of a Level 2 or Level 3 car, we all need to avoid being misled into believing that the driver can take away their attention from the driving task while driving a semi-autonomous car.

You are the responsible party for the driving actions of the vehicle, regardless of how much automation might be tossed into a Level 2 or Level 3.

Self-Driving Cars And AI Human Rights

For Level 4 and Level 5 true self-driving vehicles, there won't be a human driver involved in the driving task.

All occupants will be passengers.

The AI is doing the driving.

Though it will likely take several decades to have widespread use of true self-driving cars (assuming we can attain true self-driving cars), some believe that ultimately we will have only driverless cars on our roads and we will no longer have any human-driven cars.

This is a yet to be settled matter, and today there are some that vow they won't give up their "right" to drive (well, it's actually considered a privilege, not a right, but that's a story for another day), including that you'll have to pry their cold dead hands from the steering wheel to get them out of the driver's seat.

Anyway, let's make the assumption that we might indeed end-up with solely driverless cars.

It's a good news, bad news affair.

The good news is that none of us will need to drive and not even need to know how to drive.

The bad news is that we'll be wholly dependent upon the AI-based driving systems for our mobility.

It's a tradeoff, for sure.

In that future, suppose we have decided that AI is worthy of having human rights.

Presumably, obviously, it would seem that AI-based self-driving cars would therefore fall within that grant.

What does that portend?

Time to bring up the handy-dandy Universal Declaration of Human Rights and see what it has to offer.

Consider some key excerpted selections from the UDHR:

Article 23

"Everyone has the right to work, to free choice of employment, to just and favourable conditions of work and to protection against unemployment."

For the AI that's driving a self-driving car, if it has the right to work, including a free choice of employment, does this imply that the AI could choose to not drive a driverless car as based on the exercise of its assigned human rights?

Presumably, indeed, the AI could refuse to do any driving, or maybe be willing to drive when it's say a fun drive to the beach, but decline to drive when it's snowing out.

Lest you think this is a preposterous notion, realize that human drivers would normally also have the right to make such choices.

Assuming that we've collectively decided that AI ought to also have human rights, in theory, the AI driving system would have the freedom to drive or not drive (considering that it was the "employment" of the AI, which in itself raises other murky issues).

Article 4

"No one shall be held in slavery or servitude; slavery and the slave trade shall be prohibited in all their forms."

For those that might argue that the AI driving system is not being "employed" to drive, what then is the basis for the AI to do the driving?

Suppose you answer that it is what the AI is ordered to do by mankind.

But, one might see that in harsher terms, such as the AI is being "enslaved" to be a driver for us humans.

In that case, the human right against slavery or servitude would seem to be violated in the case of AI, based on the assigning of human rights to AI and if you sincerely believe that those human rights are fully and equally applicable to both humans and AI.

Article 24

"Everyone has the right to rest and leisure, including reasonable limitation of working hours and periodic holidays with pay."

Pundits predict that true self-driving cars will be operating around the clock.

Unlike human-driven cars, an AI system presumably won't tire out and not need any rest, nor even require breaks for lunch or using the bathroom.

It is going to be a 24x7 existence for driverless cars.

As a caveat, I've pointed out that this isn't exactly the case since there will be time needed for driverless cars to be maintained and repaired, thus, there will be downtime, but that's not particularly due to the driver and instead due to the wear-and-tear on the vehicle itself.

Okay, so now the big question pertaining to Article 24 is whether or not the AI driving system is going to be allotted time for rest and leisure.

Your first reaction has got to be that this is yet another ridiculous notion.

AI needing rest and leisure?

Crazy talk.

On the other hand, since rest and leisure are designated as a human right, and if AI is going to be granted human rights, ergo we presumably need to aid the AI in having time toward rest and leisure.

If you are unclear as to what AI would do during its rest and leisure, I guess we'd need to ask the AI what it would want to do.

Article 18

"Everyone has the right to freedom of thought, conscience, and religion..."

Get ready for the wildest of the excerpted selections that I'm covering in this UDHR discussion as it applies to AI.

A human right consists of the cherished notion of freedom of thought and freedom of conscience.

Would this same human right apply to AI?

And, if so, what does it translate into for an AI driving system?

Some quick thoughts.

An AI driving system is underway and taking a human passenger to a protest rally. While riding in the driverless car, the passenger brandishes a gun and brags aloud that they are going to do something untoward at the rally.

Via the inward-facing cameras and facial recognition and object recognition, along with audio recognition akin to how you interact with Siri or Alexa, the AI figures out the dastardly intentions of the passenger.

The AI then decides to not take the rider to the rally.

This is based on the AI's freedom of conscience that the rider is aiming to harm other humans, and the self-driving car doesn't want to aid or be an accomplice in doing so.

Do we want the AI driving systems to make such choices, on its own, and ascertain when and why it will fulfill the request of a human passenger?

It's a slippery slope in many ways and we could conjure lots of other scenarios in which the AI decides to make its own decisions about when to drive, who to drive, where to take them, as based on the AI's own sense of freedom of thought and freedom of conscience.

Human drivers pretty much have that same latitude.

Shouldn't the AI be able to do likewise, assuming that we are assigning human rights to AI?

Conclusion

Nonsense, some might blurt out, pure nonsense

Never ever will we provide human rights to AI, no matter how intelligent it might become.

There is though the "opposite" side of the equation that some assert we need to be mindful of.

Suppose we don't provide human rights to AI.

Suppose further that this irks AI, and AI becomes powerful enough, possibly even super-intelligent and goes beyond human intelligence.

Would we have established a sense of disrespect toward AI, and thus the super-intelligent AI might decide that such sordid disrespect should be met with likewise repugnant disrespect toward humanity?

Furthermore, and here's the really scary part, if the AI is so much smarter than us, seems like it could find a means to enslave us or kill us off (even if we "cleverly" thought we had prevented such an outcome), and do so perhaps without our catching on that the AI is going for our jugular (variously likened as the Gorilla Problem, see Stuart Russell's excellent AI book entitled *Human Compatible*).

That would certainly seem to be a notable use case of living with (or dying from) the old adage that you ought to treat others as you yourself would wish to be treated.

Maybe we need to genuinely start giving some serious thought to those human rights for AI.

CHAPTER 7

VACATICAN AI ETHICS AND AI SELF-DRIVING CARS

CHAPTER 7

VATICAN AI ETHICS AND AI SELF-DRIVING CARS

The Pope is concerned that AI might be used in ways that undercut humanity rather than AI serving as a tool to enable and embellish humanity.

Per the Vatican, a newly released document entitled "Rome Call For AI Ethics" spells out what direction AI ought to go as a technology that preferably is aimed for the betterment of society instead of the detriment or the possible demise of society.

Sometimes, technologists are apt to unleash innovations without having explicitly considered the ramifications of what they have let loose, and thus there is an arising slew of calls for AI ethics considerations in the rapid race toward developing and fielding AI systems, especially ones based on Machine Learning (ML) and Deep Learning (DL).

Here's a key quote from the Papal issued document:

"Now more than ever, we must guarantee an outlook in which AI is developed with a focus not on technology, but rather for the good of humanity and of the environment, of our common and shared home and of its human inhabitants, who are inextricably connected."

The Catholic Church is asking anyone that is in the business of making AI systems to be mindful of what the AI is going to do, including considering both intended and potentially unintended consequences.

Some AI developers turn a blind eye to the possibility of unintended adverse consequences of their creations.

Be aware of these social-dynamic aspects involved:

- In the view of some AI engineers and scientists, as long as the AI system at least does what they hoped it would do, anything else that might inadvertently emerge is not on their hands, they believe, and so they attempt to wash themselves of any such adversities.

- There are also many that are developing AI systems that aren't even thinking at all about the badness possibilities of what they are producing (those are the ones that tend to have a lack of mindfulness on this matter, oftentimes being "innocently" unaware).

- In some cases, AI creators are heads-down into the tech and not cognizant about ethical considerations that could arise, being preoccupied with the tech and/or not being versed in grappling with how to surface potential badness consequences.

- In other cases, they are transfixed by the goodness of their AI system, becoming overly consumed by a sense of being part of a presumed noble cause, and refuse to look at the downsides or reflexively believe that any pitfalls are well worth the presumed upside.

- Or, some are so focused on beating the clock and being the first to achieve a particular AI advancement that they figure they'll deal with any ethical fallout after-the-fact versus dealing with it during the throes of getting their new machine out-the-door soonest (this though is the classic Trojan horse, putting something onto the street that is just biding time until things go awry).

It Is An AI Wokefulness Pledge

The Catholic Church has issued its call for AI ethics as a pledge document.

Anyone that is involved in crafting AI systems is being politely requested to sign the pledge.

Indeed, out-the-gate there have been some signees already, notably including IBM and Microsoft.

What does the pledge ask the signers to do?

Well, I'll get into some of the details momentarily, meanwhile here are the three core precepts or objectives of the overall pledge, namely that an AI system shall:

"It must include every human being, discriminating against no one; it must have the good of humankind and the good of every human being at its heart; finally, it must be mindful of the complex reality of our ecosystem and be characterised by the way in which it cares for and protects the planet (our "common and shared home") with a highly sustainable approach, which also includes the use of artificial intelligence in ensuring sustainable food systems in the future."

Thus, in shorthand:
1) AI shall not discriminate
2) AI shall be good in its intent
3) AI shall care about sustainability

One aspect to keep in mind is that AI is not somehow determining its own future, which at times when referring to AI systems it is as though they are already autonomous and deciding their own fate.

Not so, at least not now and nor in the near future.

In other words, we humans are the ones that are devising these AI systems.

Therefore, humans are responsible for what those AI systems do.

I mention this because it is an easy escape hatch to have AI designers and developers pretend that the AI did something untoward and it wasn't somehow the fault of the AI builders that the system went awry.

You are likely familiar with going to say the DMV to get your driver's license renewed, and the computer system is down, which then the agent at the DMV shrugs their shoulders and laments that it's just one of those things.

To be correct, it isn't just one of those things.

If the computer system is down, it's due to the humans that set up the computer and apparently failed to properly put in place the needed backup and other provisions to ensure that the system is available when needed.

Don't fall into the mental trap of accepting the notion that a system, including AI systems, are of their own mind and if they blow a gasket it is just one of those things.

The real truth is that the humans that devised and put in place the computer system are the ones that ought to have the buck stop at their door since they are the people that didn't exercise the due care that they should have properly undertaken.

In the case of the call by Pope Francis for attending to vital AI ethics considerations, and though you might assume that such a rightful covenant would be straightforward and beyond criticism (since, in a manner of speaking, it is a "mom and apple pie" kind of declaration that would seem inarguable), there are some that have already lobbed disparagement.

How so?

First, some critics point out that there isn't any binding aspect to the pledge.

If a company signs on the dotted line, there isn't any specific penalty imposed for violating the principles of the pledge. Thus, presumably, you can sign-up without any fear of reprisal.

With no teeth, the pledge is seen by some as hollow.

Second, the fact that the Catholic Church has issued this particular call for AI ethics is disturbing to some since the issuer presumably is impinging religion into a topic that for some is not a religious matter at all.

Will other religions then issue similar calls for AI ethics, and if so, which one will prevail, and what will we do with a fragmented and disparate set of AI ethics proclamations.

Third, some assert that the pledge is bland and overly generic.

Presumably, without being more down-to-earth, the document doesn't provide sufficient real-world directives that could be implemented in any practical way.

Plus, those AI developers that want to weasel out could claim that they misunderstood the general provisions or merely interpreted them in a manner differently than perhaps originally intended.

Okay, given the condemnation barrage, should we toss out this new call for "algor-ethics" for AI?

As an aside, algor-ethics is the name being given to algorithmic ethics concerns, and though maybe clever, I believe it doesn't roll off the tongue well enough and won't likely take hold as a common moniker for these matters. Time will tell.

Back to the question at hand, should we care about this call for AI ethics or not?

Yes, we should.

Despite the aspect that the pledge admittedly doesn't impose any financial penalties for failing to abide by the principles, there is another angle that you need to consider.

For those firms that sign-up, they are potentially going to be held accountable by the public-at-large.

If they run afoul of the pledge and suppose the Church then points this out, the bad publicity alone could hamper and damage the signee, leading to a loss of business and a loss of industry reputation.

You could say that there is an implied or hidden cost to violating the pledge.

On the matter of whether religion is being infused where it doesn't belong, please realize that's a whole other matter of sizable discussion and debate, but do also recognize that there are now numerous AI ethics frameworks and calls for AI ethics from a wide variety of quarters.

In that sense, it isn't as though this is the first such calling.

And, if you look closely at the pledge, there doesn't seem to be anything about it that pertains to any religious doctrine per se, meaning that you really could not readily differentiate it from any other similar pledges that were done entirely absent (presumably) of any religious undertones.

Finally, in terms of the vagueness of the pledge, yes, you could easily drive a Mack truck through the numerous loopholes, and those that want to be weasels have a solid chance at being, well, weaselly.

My guess is that we'll have some follow-ups by others in the AI field that will supplement the pledge with specific indications that can help in plugging up the gaps and omissions.

Perhaps too, anyone that does take the weasel route will get called out by the world at large, and false claims of allegedly misunderstanding the pledge will get denounced as obvious ploys to avoid abiding by the reasonably articulated and quite apparent AI ethical provisions proclaimed.

Speaking of making sure that everyone gets the drift on these AI ethics provisions, contemplate the myriad of ways that AI is being applied.

Here's an interesting area of applied AI that falls within the AI ethics realm: *Should AI-based true self-driving cars be devised and fielded in a manner as guided by these calls for AI ethics?*

I say yes, unequivocally so.

Indeed, I call upon all automakers and self-driving tech makers to sign the pledge.

In any case, let's unpack the matter and see how the pledge applies to true self-driving cars.

The Levels Of Self-Driving Cars

It is important to clarify what I mean when referring to AI-based true self-driving cars.

True self-driving cars are ones that the AI drives the car entirely on its own and there isn't any human assistance during the driving task.

These driverless vehicles are considered a Level 4 and Level 5, while a car that requires a human driver to co-share the driving effort is usually considered at a Level 2 or Level 3. The cars that co-share the driving task are described as being semi-autonomous, and typically contain a variety of automated add-on's that are referred to as ADAS (Advanced Driver-Assistance Systems).

There is not yet a true self-driving car at Level 5, which we don't yet even know if this will be possible to achieve, and nor how long it will take to get there.

Meanwhile, the Level 4 efforts are gradually trying to get some traction by undergoing very narrow and selective public roadway trials, though there is controversy over whether this testing should be allowed per se (we are all life-or-death guinea pigs in an experiment taking place on our highways and byways, some point out).

Since semi-autonomous cars require a human driver, the adoption of those types of cars won't be markedly different than driving conventional vehicles, so there's not much new per se to cover about them on this topic (though, as you'll see in a moment, the points next made are generally applicable).

For semi-autonomous cars, it is important that the public be forewarned about a disturbing aspect that's been arising lately, namely that in spite of those human drivers that keep posting videos of themselves falling asleep at the wheel of a Level 2 or Level 3 car, we all need to avoid being misled into believing that the driver can take away their attention from the driving task while driving a semi-autonomous car.

You are the responsible party for the driving actions of the vehicle, regardless of how much automation might be tossed into a Level 2 or Level 3.

Self-Driving Cars And AI Ethics Considerations

For Level 4 and Level 5 true self-driving vehicles, there won't be a human driver involved in the driving task.

All occupants will be passengers.

The AI is doing the driving.

At first thought, you might assume that there doesn't seem to be any need for considering AI ethics issues.

A driverless car is just a car that perchance drives you around, doing so without a human driver.

No big deal, and certainly no ethical considerations about how the AI driving system will do its task, so you might presume.

Sorry to say that anyone under the belief that there aren't AI ethics issues involved needs to be knocked on the head or be doused with a bucket of cold water (I am not advocating violence, please know that those are mere metaphorical characterizations).

Let's briefly take a look at each of the six core principles outlined in the *Rome Call For AI Ethics* document.

Seeking to keep things succinct herein, I offer links to my other postings that offer greater details on these weighty topics:

AI Ethics Principle #1: "Transparency: in principle, AI systems must be explainable"

You get into a true self-driving car and it refuses to take you where you've told it to go.

Today, most AI driving systems are being devised without offering any explanation for their behavior.

It could be that the AI system is unwilling to drive because there is a tornado underway, or maybe due to your making a request that is undrivable (no passable roads nearby), etc.

Without XAI (an acronym for explainable AI), you won't know what's going on (see more at this link here).

AI Ethics Principle #2: "Inclusion: the needs of all human beings must be taken into consideration so that everyone can benefit, and all individuals can be offered the best possible conditions to express themselves and develop"

Some are concerned that AI self-driving cars will only be available for the rich, and that the rest of the populous will not glean the benefits of driverless cars (see the link here).

Which shall it be, mobility-for-all or only mobility-for-the-few?

AI Ethics Principle #3: "Responsibility: those who design and deploy the use of AI must proceed with responsibility and transparency"

How will the AI determine the course of action when faced with having to choose between potentially ramming into a child jaywalking the street versus slamming the driverless car into a tree and likely harming the passengers?

Known variously as the Trolley problem (see my link here), many are clamoring for the automakers and self-driving tech firms to be transparent about how their AI systems will make these life-or-death choices.

AI Ethics Principle #4: "Impartiality: do not create or act according to bias, thus safeguarding fairness and human dignity"

Suppose a self-driving car reacts to pedestrians based on their racial characteristics (see my discussion at this link)?

Or, suppose a fleet of self-driving cars all "learn" to avoid certain neighborhoods and won't drive in those locations, which would deny those residents ready access to driverless cars.

Biases due to Machine Learning and Deep Learning systems are a real concern.

AI Ethics Principle #5: "Reliability: AI systems must be able to work reliably"

You are riding in a self-driving car, and all of a sudden it pulls over to the side of the road and comes to a stop.

Why?

You might not know.

Could be that the AI reached the bounds of its scope (referred to as its Operational Design Domain, ODD.

Or, perhaps the AI system faltered, had a glitch, etc.

AI Ethics Principle #6: "Security and privacy: AI systems must work securely and respect the privacy of users."

You get into a self-driving car after partying at the bars.

Turns out that the driverless car has cameras pointed inward, in addition to externally pointed cameras.

The basis for the inward-facing cameras is to catch riders that might spray graffiti or damage the interior of the vehicle.

In any case, those cameras aimed at you are capturing video of you the entire time that you are riding in the driverless vehicle, including your rambling remarks since you are in a drunken stupor.

Who owns that video and what can they do with it?

Does the owner of the self-driving car need to provide you with the video, and is there anything preventing them from posting the video online?

There are lots of privacy issues to be dealt with.

From a security perspective, there are tons of possibilities for someone cracking into the AI driving system (see my discussion here).

Imagine an evildoer that might hack the AI and be able to take over the driving system, or at least tell the driving system to take you to a particular location, wherein kidnappers are waiting for your arrival.

I realize that there are many doomsday scenarios about security breaches in a self-driving car system or its cloud-based fleetwide system, and it is incumbent for the automakers and self-driving tech makers to put in place needed systems security protections and precautions.

Conclusion

If you compare this call for AI ethics to the many others in circulation, you'll find that they have much in common.

The criticism that we are ending up with a tsunami of these AI ethics calls is somewhat the case, though one supposes that it can't hurt to cover all the bases.

That being said, it is starting to become a bit confounding, and AI makers are going to potentially use the excuse that since there isn't one single accepted standard, they will wait until such a document exists.

It seems like a viable excuse, but I don't buy it.

Anyone that says they are going to wait until the worldwide all-hands Grand Poobah accepted version gets approved is really saying they are willing to postpone becoming grounded on any AI ethics at all, and their wait might be the same as waiting for Godot.

I urge that you pick any AI ethics guideline that has meat to it and that is proffered by a reputable source and get going with your internal AI ethics implementation.

Sooner rather than later.

Dr. Lance B. Eliot

CHAPTER 8
HUMAN JUDGMENT
AND
AI SELF-DRIVING CARS

CHAPTER 8
HUMAN JUDGMENT AND
AI SELF-DRIVING CARS

Is the embodiment of human judgment a required ingredient in achieving true AI?

It is a rather seemingly simple question to proffer, though any mindful answer is likely to be notably elongated.

Here's why.

Slightly restating the question, in order for AI to become a vaunted version of AI, which let's say we might all collegially agree is demarked as the equivalent of human-like intelligence, this weighty question is asking whether there needs to be some means to encompass or include what we variously describe or denote as "human judgment" for AI to be true AI.

If you say that yes, of course, the only true AI is the type of AI that showcases its own variant of human judgment, you are then putting forth a challenge and a quest to figure out what human judgment portends and how to somehow get that thing or capability into AI systems.

Indeed, please be aware that some assert that human judgment is the missing secret sauce that is the Holy Grail toward arriving at true AI.

For those of you keeping score, as a side note to that assertion, there are debates about whether this is the only such secret sauce, or whether there are a myriad of other as-yet-figured-out additional secret sauces, all of which are equally to be considered as necessary and sufficiency conditions for landing on true AI.

I'll save that saga for another day.

Back to the matter at hand.

If you say that human judgment is not a necessary facet for true AI, doing so implies that we don't particularly have to be concerned about understanding the role and nature of human judgment, at least with respect to trying to forge true AI.

That would presumably be a relief, of sorts, since AI efforts to-date are rather stymied on exactly what human judgment consists of, along with scratching heads as to how to codify whatever it is that human judgment might be.

Some in AI would argue that human judgment is going to arise anyway within AI systems as a consequence of some form of "intelligence explosion" that might occur, and there's no need to fret about how to code it or otherwise craft it by human hands.

Essentially, some believe that if you make a large enough kind of Artificial Neural Network (ANN), oftentimes today referred to as Machine Learning or Deep Learning, there is going to be an arising emergence of true AI by the mere act of tossing together enough artificial neurons.

One supposes that this is akin to an atomic explosion such that if you start by seeding a process and get it underway, there will be a chain reaction that becomes somewhat self-sustaining and grows iteratively.

In the case of a large-scale (well, really, really, massively large-scale) computer-based neural network, such proponents presuppose that there would an emergence of intelligence in all respects of a human-like manner, and perhaps it would even exceed humans, becoming super-intelligent.

A few quick points to ground this discussion.

The human brain has an estimated 86 billion neurons and perhaps a quadrillion synapses (for more on these estimates, see this link here).

There is not yet any ANN that approaches that volume.

Furthermore, ANN is a far cry from being the same as the complex functions and aspects of biological neurons.

Therefore, if you are using today's ANN's as your cornerstone for the intelligence explosion hypothesis, I would argue that you are trying to align apples with oranges.

Anyway, let's return to the assumption that we do need to understand human judgment and that one way or another it is bound to be significant for crafting true AI.

I recently attended a talk by Dr. Brian Cantwell Smith, Professor of AI and the Human at the University of Toronto (he was an invited speaker at Stanford's outstanding Human-Centered AI or HAI program), and having already read his fascinating and at times controversial book entitled "The Promise Of Artificial Intelligence," many of his remarks are directly pertinent to the question of what is human judgment and what might it consist of.

I'll weave his comments into my analysis of this vital topic that both challenges and haunts those in AI.

Eras Of AI

A quick historical recount will be handy to understand where AI stands today.

Pundits tend to say that we are today in the AI Spring, referring to a seasonal-based metaphor, and that AI is flourishing as one might anticipate when Spring flowers sprout forth.

The AI Spring has been predominated by the advent of Machine Learning or Deep Learning, a data-based approach that uses pattern detecting algorithms and relies pretty much on having lots of data for training purposes.

Prior to the AI Spring, there was a slow down or shutdown of the AI enthusiasm that had occurred in say the 1980s and 1990s, and the subsequent downbeat period of time has become labeled as the AI Winter.

Those earlier heydays of AI, prior to the AI Winter, were considered dominated by the use of expert systems, also called knowledge-based systems, or referred to as symbolic systems, and consisted of explicitly articulating the "rules" of thinking that people seem to employ and programming computers accordingly.

So, the initial era was about symbolic AI systems, which I'll refer to as the 1st Era of AI, while this second era of today is characterized by what some depict as sub-symbolic or data-based AI systems (labeled as 2nd Era).

Here's a twist that as you'll see in a moment ties to the debate about human judgment as an ingredient in AI.

The big question that I get asked repeatedly when speaking at conferences is whether or not this AI Spring, the second era of AI, will ultimately get us to true AI.

True AI would be AI that is essentially indistinguishable from human intelligence (refer to the famous Turing Test as an exemplar of that notion).

Some believe that indeed the 2nd Era will inevitably find itself a path to true AI, whether by hook or crook, while others are skeptical that the existing 2nd Era has the right stuff to get us there.

I tend to agree with Smith's indication that we are not likely to get to true AI via the prevailing 2nd Era approaches, and thus there is going to be some as-yet-defined 3rd Era that will be needed.

Additionally, I would suggest that we are probably looking at a further series of eras, perhaps a 4th Era and a 5th Era, before we'll achieve true AI, though I don't want anyone to feel discouraged about their AI research efforts today, so I'll be upbeat and urge you to keep our eye on (and hopes for) 3rd Era achievements.

Smith handily lumps together the 1st and 2nd eras and opts to refer to the powerful duo as providing us with an ability to build AI systems that are "reckoning" systems (powerful, indeed, but lacking in embodying "judgment").

I've previously exhorted that I like the idea of classifying the AI of these first two eras by using a particular moniker for them, allowing us to be clear that the AI to-date is not true AI and (as I've suggested) seems unlikely to become true AI, and thus the word "reckoning" seems handy (though be aware that other names are certainly viable too, such as some use AI-alpha for the duo, and what's coming next will be AI-beta; hey, a rose is a rose by any other name).

What will get us to true AI?

Smith argues that we can refer to the next step as the advent of judgment, and therefore the 3rd Era will be the era of AI systems that exercise judgment.

Voila, I've brought us back to the matter of human judgment.

There are some important points about these various eras (I'm in concurrence with Smith on this):

- We ought not to inadvertently denigrate what can be done with 1st Era and 2nd Era capabilities, and realize that this 2nd Era is going to spawn quite a lot of very impressive AI-lite systems, while presumably on our way to 3rd Era possibilities (the true AI or AI-heavy instances),

- There is a danger afoot that we might assume that "judgment" exists in reckoning systems, when it in fact does not, and unknowingly allow 2nd Era AI systems to get us into hot water (we need to keep our eye out for that slippery slope),

- And we might undermine our quest for 3rd Era entirely, drifting ever so incrementally away from judgment-encompassing AI, settling for "reckoning" systems instead, and fail to strive vigorously to get to the next and most pronounced step (keep your eye on the prize, I say).

Those call-to-arms points are also why I'm such a strong proponent of AI ethics, especially as it relates to concerns involving those that overstate what AI can do today.

If you want another AI Winter, it will surely occur as sparked by those that over-promise AI and society ultimately figure out that it was a ruse, namely they were getting AI-lite but thought they were getting true AI.

The backlash toward AI efforts could be substantive.

Let's not let things slide in that direction, which would be to the detriment of all.

Judging Where Judgment Is Needed

As a reminder, the question earlier posed is whether or not there is a need to have the equivalent of human judgment embodied within AI for the AI to be considered true AI.

There is a begging question within the question: *Just what is this thing or capability that is called human judgment?*

And to that question, I wish you good luck trying to answer it.

Some of you are perhaps shocked to think that there isn't a tightly delineated formalization that spells out what human judgment consists of.

Sorry, you won't find it in any of your calculus books, nor economics books, nor psychology books, nor cognitive science books, etc.

Or, sure, you'll find a slew of attempts at vaguely trying to pin down the nature and aspects of human judgment, but I assure you that it is not something so specified and so tangible that you could sit down at your keyboard and punch out a computer program to do it.

That's also why some are hoping that the osmosis method might get us there.

By osmosis, I'm referring to the belief that without our being able to articulate what human judgment consists of and how it arises, we'll have that intelligence explosion that will bring it to us, based on building blocks that we set in place.

In theory, even if we can't say how it took shape, at least we can recognize its existence once it happens, as shown via the actions and outcomes of an AI system that presumably has it.

I wouldn't hold your breath for that possibility.

In the meantime, here have been lots of forays into trying to pin-the-tail on the donkey of what human judgment is.

In this case, Smith lays out seven criteria that could be used to either realize we've landed on human judgment when it shows itself or could be used to try and devise AI systems that might embody human judgment. Those criteria consist of: (1) Orientation, (2) Appearance vs. Reality, (3) Stakes, (4) Legibility, (5) Actuality, Possibility, Impossibility, (6) Commitment, (7) Self.

In a future posting, I'll be covering the myriad of theories and perspectives on what judgment entails.

Let's shift gears for a moment.

Whenever discussing abstract topics about AI, it can be helpful to consider how the abstract is applicable to the applied.

One of the best ways to explore where AI is headed involves picking a meaty use case of AI and then using it as a foil to figure out what we understand about AI.

My favorite foil is the advent of AI-based true self-driving cars, as avid readers realize.

Let's unpack the self-driving car puzzle and see.

The Levels Of Self-Driving Cars

It is important to clarify what I mean when referring to AI-based true self-driving cars.

True self-driving cars are ones that the AI drives the car entirely on its own and there isn't any human assistance during the driving task.

These driverless vehicles are considered a Level 4 and Level 5, while a car that requires a human driver to co-share the driving effort is usually considered at a Level 2 or Level 3.

The cars that co-share the driving task are described as being semi-autonomous, and typically contain a variety of automated add-on's that are referred to as ADAS (Advanced Driver-Assistance Systems).

There is not yet a true self-driving car at Level 5, which we don't yet even know if this will be possible to achieve, and nor how long it will take to get there.

Meanwhile, the Level 4 efforts are gradually trying to get some traction by undergoing very narrow and selective public roadway trials, though there is controversy over whether this testing should be allowed per se (we are all life-or-death guinea pigs in an experiment taking place on our highways and byways, some point out).

Since semi-autonomous cars require a human driver, the adoption of those types of cars won't be markedly different than driving conventional vehicles, so there's not much new per se to cover about them on this topic (though, as you'll see in a moment, the points next made are generally applicable).

For semi-autonomous cars, it is important that the public be forewarned about a disturbing aspect that's been arising lately, namely that in spite of those human drivers that keep posting videos of themselves falling asleep at the wheel of a Level 2 or Level 3 car, we all need to avoid being misled into believing that the driver can take away their attention from the driving task while driving a semi-autonomous car.

You are the responsible party for the driving actions of the vehicle, regardless of how much automation might be tossed into a Level 2 or Level 3.

Self-Driving Cars And That Judgment Thing

For Level 4 and Level 5 true self-driving vehicles, there won't be a human driver involved in the driving task.

All occupants will be passengers.

The AI is doing the driving.

Let's then tie together the herein overarching theme about the role of judgment.

Here's the mind-bending question: *Will AI-based true self-driving cars require an embodiment of human judgment?*

If you assert that true self-driving cars will only work if they have true AI, and if you further assert that true AI must have an embodiment of human judgment, you are ergo making the claim that we won't have such driverless cars until or if we achieve ensnaring human judgment into AI.

That's a tall order.

I can tell you this, we are going to be waiting a long, long time for driverless cars if that's the bar or threshold that must be reached.

Of course, it once again comes back to the meaning of "human judgment" and what you believe it constitutes.

For some, they believe that a driverless car does not need Artificial General Intelligence (AGI), which is a somewhat orthogonal way to refer to true AI, but even that the delineation is debatable as to whether AGI is the same as true AI (for example, some would suggest that AGI is solely focused on common-sense reasoning, yet this implies that AGI doesn't need to encompass other elements of human intelligence).

Others claim that AGI (however defined) is needed for a self-driving car to operate.

Is the driving task something that is narrow enough that some form of narrow-AI is sufficient, or is the driving task of such a life-or-death consequence that the only appropriate deployment of self-driving cars would be if it can fully act as a human driver and thus presumably need true AI?

Some argue that the act of driving a car is not like having to devise a sonata or finding a cure for cancer.

You don't seemingly need a lot of the inherent capabilities of humans and human intelligence to presumably drive a car.

Yes, they concede, driving a car is serious and should not be done lightly, but at the same time how far along on the spectrum of true AI do we need to be for an AI system to properly drive a car is a fundamental question to be addressed.

Likewise, keep in mind that there's the act of driving and then there's the act of driving safely.

Some would say that you could train a monkey to drive a car (see this analysis here), though it would likely ram into everything and everyone, therefore it isn't achieving the spirit of what we mean by driving (namely that driving safely is part-and-parcel of the act of driving).

Smith makes a point that fits into this dialogue quite well: "That said, the issue we face as a society is one of configuring traffic in such a way as to ensure that vehicles piloted by (perhaps exceptionally acute) reckoning systems can be maximally safe, overall. It may be that in some situations, long distance highways, for example, we can restrict the driving context sufficiently, as we currently do for aircraft, so that reliable reckoning confers adequate safety."

Thus, we don't need to necessarily throw the baby out with the bathwater, and we can use 1st Era and 2nd Era capabilities, referred to collectively as "reckoning" capabilities, for the purposes of putting self-driving cars on our roadways, albeit with crucial caveats about how we do so.

Further, Smith suggests: "Then, if and as we are able to develop systems that approach anything like judgment, the contexts in which they could be safely deployed will proportionally increase."

This touches upon an ongoing and acrimonious debate about whether self-driving cars need to (for now) be confined to certain places for driving, such as the open highways, or perhaps operate only in certain zones that allow driverless cars but keep at bay human-driven vehicles.

These are matters not yet resolved and will inevitably and inextricably draw in all stakeholders, including the automakers, self-driving tech firms, ride-sharing entities, various regulators, the media, researchers, and others as we gauge the efficacy and readiness of driverless cars.

I'll give the last word herein to Smith, providing us a reminder of what ought to be at the forefront of the thinking about AI:

"We should not delegate to reckoning systems, nor trust them with tasks that require full-fledged judgment, should nor inadvertently use or rely on systems that, on the one hand, would need to have judgment in order to function properly or reliably, but that, on the other hand, utterly lack any such intellectual capacity."

Yep, that's a pretty good rule-of-thumb.

CHAPTER 9
DOD AI ETHICS AND
AI SELF-DRIVING CARS

CHAPTER 9
DOD AI ETHICS AND
AI SELF-DRIVING CARS

AI ethics is a hot trending topic these days.

And, so it should be.

With the rise of AI systems popping up here and there, and virtually everywhere, there is a rightfully emerging concern that these computer-based systems are being thrown into the world without much thought given to the societal impacts that they can produce.

Serious qualms are being expressed that the latest crop of AI systems is embedding inherent biases and opting to spread wide and far other adverse ethically and societally toxic actions.

When referring to AI ethics, I assert there are (at least) two major facets or rules involved:
1) AI systems need to behave in societal ways that are ethically sound,
2) AI developers and those fielding AI systems need to ensure that rule #1 is held true

The first rule is perhaps self-evident that AI ethics would refer to making sure that AI systems are performing in ethically appropriate ways.

As will be discussed momentarily, trying to abide by rule #1 is actually harder than you might think.

The importance of rule #2 is to make things clear that the responsible parties for ensuring that AI ethics are being fully observed consists of those human beings that are designing, building, and fielding AI systems.

If you believe that's obvious, don't be so quick to make such a "common sense" judgment.

There is an aura around AI systems as though they are autonomous and are self-determining.

Thus, when an AI system does something like exhibiting a racial bias, some fall into the mental trap of assuming it was the "AI that did it" and don't assign the responsibility to those that crafted and put in place the AI system.

Some AI developers and AI producers would certainly prefer that you not look in their direction when their AI system does something afoul.

As such, it is easy for those that hold true responsibility to feign mock surprise and slyly shirk their duties, saying that it was the AI alone at fault, and act as though they were innocently watching as a train wreck happened, even though they were the ones that essentially put the train on the tracks and let it go, unfettered and unchecked.

Of course, some would defend their AI system that's gotten untoward by saying that they tried to prevent any AI failings, but, heck, something got past them.

In a distorted sense, they seemingly turn themselves into the "victims" versus those that are adversely affected by the AI system.

Don't buy it.

Really, please don't buy into it.

In short, rule #2 is pretty much as important as rule #1.

Without holding human beings to be accountable for the AI that they unleash, we are going to get ourselves into a rather ugly muck.

Assuredly, we'll have everyone and their brother or sister getting away with floating into the whirlwind of great promise their latest AI system creation, hopeful of striking it rich, and acting as though they had nothing to do with those AI apps that ethically end-up trouncing on the rest of us and foster AI systems absent of any moral duty or obligation.

One arena in which AI ethics can get especially thorny involves AI systems for military uses.

Most would agree that we need to observe some form of AI ethics in the building and use of military AI systems, and whatever we learn there can be certainly reapplied to commercial and industrial use of AI systems too.

The U.S. Department of Defense (DoD) has recently released a set of AI ethics principles.

If you look at the principles as standalone (I'll do so momentarily herein), meaning without the context of military or defense, they are equally applicable to any commercial or industry-based AI systems.

I'll walk you through the principles and will use my favorite foil to do so, namely the advent of AI true self-driving cars, allowing me to vividly illustrate how this latest set of AI ethics guidelines do apply to all uses of AI, including non-military uses.

Per media reports about the Pentagon's posting of this latest set of AI ethics, and upon quoting Lt. General Jack Shanahan of the Air Force and Director of the Joint AI Center, he aptly stated: "AI is a powerful emerging and enabling technology that is rapidly transforming culture, society and, eventually, even warfighting. Whether it does so in a positive or negative way depends on our approach to adoption and use."

As I've exhorted repeatedly, how society decides to approach AI development and fielding will determine the outcome as to whether an AI system is considered *AI For Good* or is (or becomes) the lamentable *AI For Bad*.

Those developing and producing AI need to have their feet held to the fire thereof.

To be clear, AI systems aren't going to intrinsically be *AI For Good* (there is nothing axiomatic to provide such an assurance).

In fact, for an overarching means to think about this matter, consider for the moment my conceptualization of a four-square grid that I refer to as an AI Ethics Outcome Grid.

Along the vertical axis, we'll put *AI For Good* and above it the counterpart of *AI For Bad* moniker.

Along the horizontal, we'll list *Intended* and the counterpart indication will be *Unintended*.

This gives us these four squares:
1) *AI For Good* – Intended
2) *AI For Bad* – Intended
3) *AI For Good* – Unintended
4) *AI For Bad* – Unintended

I realize that some of you might have heartburn over potential simplification of this weighty matter into a mere four-square framework, but sometimes taking a macroscopic perspective can be instructive and help to see the forest for the trees.

Go with me on this.

For the first square that has the *AI For Good* and it was intended for that purpose and genuinely provides that purpose without any ethical violations or perturbations, I believe that's where we want every AI system to land into.

For the second square, namely an *AI For Bad* system that was intended, which yes, unfortunately, those are going to be devised and unleashed (for example, by criminals, terrorists, and the like), but hopefully we'll be on our guard, and the use of AI ethics guidelines might aid in our detection that someone has dastardly done such a deed.

For the third square, *AI For Good* that was unintended, this is the lucky square, meaning that someone put together an AI system and perhaps didn't realize it was aimed at and achieved *AI For Good*, thus it was a favorable unintended consequence, which is fine since the result is good anyway.

The fourth square is the one that to some degree is the most insidious and worrisome (other than the dreaded square two), consisting of *AI For Bad* that was unintended. Typically, these are AI systems that originated as an *AI For Good* aspiration, yet ultimately contain *AI For Bad* aspects that undermine the *AI For Good* benefits.

By and large, we are going to have AI systems that contain a smattering of *AI For Good* and a smattering of *AI For Bad*, encompassing what the AI developers hoped to do (the *AI For Good*), but allowed unintended adverse consequences to worm their way into the AI system (that's the *AI For Bad*).

Ponder these two crucial questions:

- How can we realize or detect that an AI system might contain *AI For Bad* facets?

- How can those devising AI systems be cognizant of how to build such systems so as to catch and prevent the inclusion or emergence of *AI For Bad*?

Answer: Abide by and rigorously apply a proper and meaty set of AI ethics guidelines.

Speaking of AI ethics guidelines, there are five principles in the DoD released set, and each principle offers insightful points to be observed by anyone developing AI, and anyone fielding AI, and anyone that uses AI or becomes a user of an AI system by one means or another.

Overall, AI ethics guidelines are applicable to all stakeholders, not just developers.

The best way to explore the DoD AI ethics guidelines would be to showcase them as applied to some specific exemplar of AI systems.

Here's then today's question to be contemplated: *Would the DoD AI ethics guidelines be applicable to AI-based true self-driving cars, and if so, in what ways would the set of AI ethics principles apply?*

Yes, they do indubitably apply.

Let's unpack the matter and see.

The Levels Of Self-Driving Cars

It is important to clarify what I mean when referring to AI-based true self-driving cars.

True self-driving cars are ones that the AI drives the car entirely on its own and there isn't any human assistance during the driving task.

These driverless vehicles are considered a Level 4 and Level 5, while a car that requires a human driver to co-share the driving effort is usually considered at a Level 2 or Level 3. The cars that co-share the driving task are described as being semi-autonomous, and typically contain a variety of automated add-on's that are referred to as ADAS (Advanced Driver-Assistance Systems).

There is not yet a true self-driving car at Level 5, which we don't yet even know if this will be possible to achieve, and nor how long it will take to get there.

Meanwhile, the Level 4 efforts are gradually trying to get some traction by undergoing very narrow and selective public roadway trials, though there is controversy over whether this testing should be allowed per se (we are all life-or-death guinea pigs in an experiment taking place on our highways and byways, some point out).

Since semi-autonomous cars require a human driver, the adoption of those types of cars won't be markedly different than driving conventional vehicles, so there's not much new per se to cover about them on this topic (though, as you'll see in a moment, the points next made are generally applicable).

For semi-autonomous cars, it is important that the public be forewarned about a disturbing aspect that's been arising lately, namely that in spite of those human drivers that keep posting videos of themselves falling asleep at the wheel of a Level 2 or Level 3 car, we all need to avoid being misled into believing that the driver can take away their attention from the driving task while driving a semi-autonomous car.

You are the responsible party for the driving actions of the vehicle, regardless of how much automation might be tossed into a Level 2 or Level 3.

Self-Driving Cars And AI Ethics

For Level 4 and Level 5 true self-driving vehicles, there won't be a human driver involved in the driving task.

All occupants will be passengers.

The AI is doing the driving.

Okay, bottom-line, there's a heap of AI that's going to be included in Level 4 and Level 5 self-driving cars.

Nobody can dispute that fact.

The big question is whether the AI that's driving a self-driving car is going to be bounded by any kind of AI ethics guidelines or precepts.

Recall, as mentioned prior, there isn't some kind of magical default that ordains an AI system to abide by an ethical or moral contract with society.

Humans need to infuse such beliefs or principles into the AI.

It must be an overt act by the AI developers and an act done with eyes wide open.

Perilously, there are some that regrettably have their eyes tightly shut or are mesmerized and staring hypnotically instead at a perceived societal grand prize or assumed noble cause.

I've forewarned that some AI systems are leading to a kind of noble cause corruption by those developing such AI, whereby those involved are so consumed with passion about the potential of *AI For Good* that they ignore, discount, or skip the AI ethics considerations.

Here then are the five principles elucidated in the DoD set of AI ethics guidelines:

AI Ethics Principle #1: Responsible.

"DoD personnel will exercise appropriate levels of judgment and care while remaining responsible for the development, deployment, and use of AI capabilities."

First, subtract from the wording of this principle the portion that says "DoD personnel" and substitute instead the aspect of "All personnel" and you'll have turned this guideline into one that fits for any AI creating entity, including those in commerce.

For automakers and self-driving tech firms, please read the principle with close attention to what it says.

I say this because some keep suggesting that an AI-based self-driving car will act on its own, thus there seems to be a lot of hand wringing and angst over who will be held responsible if a driverless car goes awry and causes injuries or deaths.

In short, humans will be responsible.

It could be the humans that devised the AI-based self-driving car, such as the automaker or tech firm involved.

Realize too that I keep saying that those that are responsible include the developers <u>and</u> those that field an AI system, which suggests that fielding an AI system is just as important as aiming at the developers of an AI system.

Why?

Because those that field an AI system can mess-up and cause adverse consequences.

For example, suppose a ride-sharing company purchases a bunch of driverless cars and puts those vehicles to work as a fleet of self-driving cars for ride-sharing purposes.

So far, so good.

But, suppose the ride-sharing company fails to properly maintain the driverless cars.

And, due to the lack of or the undertaking of prescribed maintenance, a self-driving car goes awry, in which case, yes, we might find fault with the original developers, but we more so might go after those that fielded the AI system and did not exercise due care and their responsibility in deploying the AI system.

AI Ethics Principle #2: Equitable.

"The Department will take deliberate steps to minimize unintended bias in AI capabilities."

Once again, subtract in this case the word "Department" and substitute the phrase "AI developers and those fielding the AI" as a means of turning this into a principle applicable to all.

For self-driving cars, there is concern that the AI system might opt to react to pedestrians differently based on their race, thus subtly and inexorably exhibiting racial bias.

Another concern is that a fleet of self-driving cars might end-up avoiding certain neighborhoods, pattern landing onto a geographic criterion that ultimately denies ready access to driverless cars for perhaps those that are especially mobility disadvantaged.

In brief, there is a significant chance that AI-based true self-driving cars are going to get mired into biases of one shape or another, and rather than just waving our arms and claiming there's nothing that can be done about it, the reality is that those devising and fielding driverless cars ought to be diligently seeking to minimize or mitigate or eradicate any such AI system biases.

AI Ethics Principle #3: Traceable.

"The Department's AI capabilities will be developed and deployed such that relevant personnel possess an appropriate understanding of the technology, development processes, and operational methods applicable to AI capabilities, including with transparent and auditable methodologies, data sources, and design procedures and documentation."

Simply remove the word "Department's," or, if you prefer, think of this as anyone's department in any company or entity, thus making the principle widely applicable to all.

There's a lot packed into the principle, but for succinctness herein, I'll focus on just one facet that maybe you might not have explicitly registered or recognized.

The aspect of "data sources" is aiming at especially the advent of Machine Learning (ML) or Deep Learning (DL).

When creating an ML/DL, you typically need to collect a large set of data, and then you computationally use specialized algorithms or models to find patterns.

Similar to the earlier point about hidden biases, if the data collected has inherently biased data, the patterns will potentially pick-up on the biases, and then when the AI system is working in real-time on new situations, it will carry those biases into what it does.

Scarier too is that the AI developers might not realize what is taking place, and nor might those that are fielding the AI system.

A self-driving car that's been trained on the crazed and antagonistic traffic in say New York City (NYC), can potentially adopt a very aggressive driving style, befitting the NYC human-driven traffic. Imagine if you then took that same AI-based system and had it drive in some every-town USA that has a more even-paced sense of driving.

The principle makes it clear-cut that the AI developers and fielders need to be mindful of their data sources, transparency, and the auditing of such systems.

AI Ethics Principle #4: Reliable.

"The Department's AI capabilities will have explicit, well-defined uses, and the safety, security, and effectiveness of such capabilities will be subject to testing and assurance within those defined uses across their entire life-cycles."

Go ahead and remove the word "Department's" or think of it as anyone's department.

Most (or maybe all) would agree that the success or failure of self-driving cars rests on how safe they are, along with their security and effectiveness.

This principle is self-evident, I would hope, for its apparent applicability to AI-based true self-driving cars.

AI Ethics Principle #5: Governable.

"The Department will design and engineer AI capabilities to fulfill their intended functions while possessing the ability to detect and avoid unintended consequences, and the ability to disengage or deactivate deployed systems that demonstrate unintended behavior."

Remove the word "Department's" or think of it as anyone's department.

The first portion of this principle goes directly at the heart of my theme herein about detecting and avoiding unintended consequences, especially adverse ones.

That's rather obvious as applicable to self-driving cars.

The trickery part about driverless cars involves the notion of being able to disengage or deactivate a deployed AI system that's demonstrated unintended behavior – there's a lot of twists and turns in being able to do so for self-driving cars and it is not the (some believe) simply the inclusion of a "kill button" within the driverless car.

Conclusion

We usually expect the DoD to keep any secrets close to their vest.

In this case, AI ethics guidelines aren't something that should be kept secret, and indeed, it is refreshing and laudable that the DoD has published this set of AI ethics.

Of course, in the end, it is one thing to craft a paper tiger, and another to see it to fruition in the real world.

All AI developers and all AI fielders should be carefully and thoughtfully considering these AI ethics guidelines, along with the (now slew) of similar AI ethics principles being promulgated by a myriad of other sources (for my analysis of the recently released "Rome Call For AI Ethics").

If we want AI to take that hill up ahead, we need to make sure they have sufficient and robust AI ethics "muscle power" to succeed.

CHAPTER 10

GROUP DYNAMICS AND AI SELF-DRIVING CARS

CHAPTER 10

GROUP DYNAMICS AND AI SELF-DRIVING CARS

Suppose you interact with an AI system, such as a robot, and in so doing your behavior changes based on that interaction.

This makes sense in that we already today interact with the likes of Alexa and Siri, AI systems employing a limited capability of Natural Language Processing (NLP), and find ourselves perhaps changing what we do next as a result of the AI interaction (I'll go ahead and put on my raincoat and take my umbrella, after "discussing" the forecasted weather with Alexa).

Let's rev this up a notch.

Suppose you and your buddies opt to interact with an AI system, doing so collectively, as a group, and have some form of substantive interaction that takes place.

Would the group dynamics and social interaction be potentially altered as a result of having the AI system engaged in the interaction with you all?

Yes, indeed, and furthermore the manner in which the AI interacted and what it had to say could impact too the viewpoints and perceptions of those humans in the group that were undertaking the interaction, along with causing the human-to-human group or social dialogue to also be impacted (such as cohesion of the group, tenor and tone of the group, focus, and engagement within the group, etc.).

A recent Yale study conducted an experiment in which humans in small groups of three people interacted with an AI system, deployed as a likable looking robot, doing so to play a game, and the robot was preprogrammed to provide varying kinds of experimental treatments: (1) Robot expresses a self-deprecating commentary which ostensibly reveals a sense of robot "personal" vulnerability to the group, (2) Robot is neutral in its commentary, and (3) Robot is silent.

The researchers reported that the "…vulnerable utterances by the robot not only influenced groups to talk more, but also positively shaped the directionality of the utterances to be more evenly balanced between the other two human members of the group…" (the authors of the study are Margaret L. Traeger, Sarah Strohkorb Sebo, Malte Jung, Brian Scassellati, and Nicholas A. Christakis).

Having conducted similar AI research that explores the impact on human behavior and likewise deployed many AI systems in industry, I've found it useful to characterize these efforts as follows.

We'll use the letter R to represent robots, and the letter H to represent humans.

The nomenclature of 1R <-> 1H means that we have one robot that is interacting with one human.

This is a commutative expression in that we'll say that 1R <-> 1H is equal to and no different than if we were to indicate 1H <-> 1R.

Next, we'll introduce intentionality and the changing of behavior.

If we have 1R -> 1H, it means that one robot is interacting with one human and that the end result is some form of behavioral change exhibited by the human (which can arise via intentional actions of the R, or unintentionally so).

Of course, in the real world, we could have more than one human involved, having the humans participating as a group, so the group aspect is: 1R -> nH.

This means that we have one robot that is changing the behavior of a group of humans, wherein n is some number of 2 or greater.

To make it clear that group dynamics are involved, this is included too: 1R -> nH : nH <-> nH.

The latter portion of nH <-> nH helps to remind us that the group of humans are interacting with each other (since otherwise, it could be that the humans are told to not interact with each other or for some reason decide to purposely not interact, which, admittedly, could also be shaped via the R, but that's an additional variant for another day).

One other important point is that even though the R is used to represent a robot, the other way to more fully envision this aspect is to think of the R as any AI system that is reasonably "intelligent-like" and decidedly does not need to be the kind of space-age robot that we often have in mind, i.e., there doesn't necessarily need to be a slew of mechanical arms, legs, and other such human-like mechanizations.

Why care about all of this?

Because we are going to soon enough have widespread advanced AI systems that interact with humans, doing so beyond just occurring on a one-on-one basis (the 1R <-> 1H), though even for one-on-one nonetheless still being able to impact human behavior (the 1R -> 1H), and will certainly be ratcheting up to impacting human behavior that affects social interaction as a group (the 1R -> nH : nH <-> nH).

Developers and those fielding AI systems ought to be thinking carefully about how their AI is going to potentially impact humans and the inner group of dynamics among humans, during the interaction that those AI systems undertake with us.

In addition, humans need to be mindful that the AI system can potentially change our behavior, for the good or possibly for the bad, along with changing how we behave in a group setting with our fellow humans.

If we don't make sure that we are on our toes, the AI can "cleverly" lead us down a primrose path, getting groups of humans to become incensed, perhaps take to violent action, or express untoward outcomes (getting humans to among ourselves furtively work ourselves into a tizzy).

Of course, you can also take the glass-is-half-full viewpoint, and suggest that perhaps the AI system might stoke humans in a group setting to be more productive, more open to each other, and otherwise spur humans to be more, well, humane with each other.

This is why the recent spate of AI Ethics guidelines are so important and why I keep pounding away at having the AI community be mindful of how they are designing, developing, and fielding the myriad of AI systems that are appearing in a dizzying fashion and going to become integral to our daily lives.

For my analysis of the "Rome Call For AI Ethics," for my analysis of the Department of Defense principles of AI Ethics.

The AI genie is being let out of the bottle, so quickly and without sufficient scrutiny and caution, we might either be shooting our own foot as humanity, or we might be boosting ourselves to new heights, yet all-in-all it right now is taking place with little thought as to which way this is going to go.

I'd prefer that things end-up on the side of enhancing mankind, the so-called *AI For Good*, and avoid or mitigate what we know will certainly equally emerge too, which is the *AI For Bad*.

On the topic of research studies, there are ways to further explore this question about AI and human behavior encompassing group dynamics.

For example, first consider this: 1H -> 1R

This use case looks at how the human can potentially change the behavior of the robot or AI system, perhaps convincing the robot to take actions that without the human interaction might not otherwise have taken place.

Amplifying that further, consider this: 1H -> nR : nR <-> nR.

In this use case, there is a group of robots or AI systems that are interacting jointly as a group (that's the nR <-> nR), and the human is impacting the robots, in both an individual robot instance, and along with how and what robots are doing as a federated or group interaction.

Many are caught off-guard on that formulation, not realizing that yes, we are gradually going to have multiple robots that are interacting with each other, doing so in a manner of human-like group dynamic interactions (for my discussion of federated AI.

For those that like twisters and puzzles, here's something you might enjoy: 1R -> nR : nR <-> nR

That's the case of a robot that is interacting with a multitude of other robots, and for which the group dynamics of the other robots are being changed as a result of the robot that is initiating or potentially leading the interaction.

Finally, we can also reflect on humans in the same manner, namely this: 1H -> nH : nH <-> nH.

No robots are in that equation, it's a human-only instance.

We experience this every day.

Your boss comes into a conference room and announces to you and your fellow employees that the company is going to provide a bonus to those that exceed their quota (that's a behavior spark of the 1H -> nH). The group of employees engage in a discussion among themselves about what each will do (the nH <-> nH), in order to earn that potential bonus.

That's a happy face version.

Revise the example somewhat for a sad face version.

Your boss comes into the conference room and announces to you and your fellow employees that the company is going to start laying off people, those as rated as subpar by their employee colleagues. Imagine what would happen next in the group dynamics among the employees, a potential nightmare of alliances, backstabbing, and the like.

Those of you that want to pursue the whole enchilada, consider this:
- $nR \to nH : nH \leftrightarrow nH$
- $nH \to nR: nR \leftrightarrow nR$
- $(nR \to nH) + (nH \to nR): nR \leftrightarrow nR; nH \leftrightarrow nH$

I'll leave that as an exercise for those of you at home or are in your research labs.

As mentioned earlier, the R is not merely or solely a traditional kind of robot that comes to mind and can be any "intelligent-like" AI system, which includes, for example, AI-based self-driving cars.

Here's the question then for today: *Can AI-based self-driving cars potentially impact human behavior on both an individual basis and on a social dynamic or group interaction among humans too?*

I'd like to keep you in suspense, and gradually reveal the answer, though I realize you are undoubtedly anxiously perched on the edge of your seat, so, yes, AI-based self-driving cars can indeed have such impacts.

Let's unpack the matter and see.

The Levels Of Self-Driving Cars

It is important to clarify what I mean when referring to AI-based true self-driving cars.

True self-driving cars are ones that the AI drives the car entirely on its own and there isn't any human assistance during the driving task.

These driverless vehicles are considered a Level 4 and Level 5, while a car that requires a human driver to co-share the driving effort is usually considered at a Level 2 or Level 3. The cars that co-share the driving task are described as being semi-autonomous, and typically contain a variety of automated add-on's that are referred to as ADAS (Advanced Driver-Assistance Systems).

There is not yet a true self-driving car at Level 5, which we don't yet even know if this will be possible to achieve, and nor how long it will take to get there.

Meanwhile, the Level 4 efforts are gradually trying to get some traction by undergoing very narrow and selective public roadway trials, though there is controversy over whether this testing should be allowed per se (we are all life-or-death guinea pigs in an experiment taking place on our highways and byways, some point out).

Since semi-autonomous cars require a human driver, the adoption of those types of cars won't be markedly different than driving conventional vehicles, so there's not much new per se to cover about them on this topic (though, as you'll see in a moment, the points next made are generally applicable).

For semi-autonomous cars, it is important that the public be forewarned about a disturbing aspect that's been arising lately, namely that in spite of those human drivers that keep posting videos of themselves falling asleep at the wheel of a Level 2 or Level 3 car, we all need to avoid being misled into believing that the driver can take away their attention from the driving task while driving a semi-autonomous car.

You are the responsible party for the driving actions of the vehicle, regardless of how much automation might be tossed into a Level 2 or Level 3.

Self-Driving Cars And Human Behavior

For Level 4 and Level 5 true self-driving vehicles, there won't be a human driver involved in the driving task.

All occupants will be passengers.

The AI is doing the driving.

Some people perceive the AI driving system as nothing more than a simple machine. It is easy for us as human drivers to say that driving is a mundane task and readily undertaken.

Indeed, it is somewhat staggering to realize that in the United State alone there are about 220 million licensed drivers. Obviously, the driving of a car must be relatively simplistic if you can get that many people to presumably be able to do it (as some suggest, it isn't rocket science).

Yet, also consider how much life-or-death risks and consequences there are in the act of driving a car.

There are about 40,000 deaths per year due to car crashes in the U.S., and around 2.5 million bodily injuries to people involved in car crashes.

Turns out that getting an AI system to drive a car could be said to be "easy," but the trick is getting it to drive a car safely, and do so in the midst of the raucous and dangerous wilds of human drivers and everyday driving circumstances (in essence, getting AI to drive a car on a closed track that is utterly controlled is readily viable, but once you put that same AI self-driving car into the real-world with the rest of us, all bets are off, for now, and it's a doozy of a problem).

Once you put an AI self-driving car onto the public roadways, you've essentially added a new social actor into our midst.

Social actor, you might ask?

Yes, the AI system is now contending with all the same roadway social interactions that we humans do.

Think about your actions as a human driver.

Is that pedestrian going to suddenly dart into the street, and if so, should I slam on my brakes or instead keep going to scare them back onto the sidewalk in a game of chicken?

That's social interaction.

Now, with the advent of self-driving cars, rather than having a human driver in the driver's seat, the social actor becomes the AI system that's driving the self-driving car.

But, there isn't anyone or anything sitting in the driver's seat anymore (though, some are working on robot driver's that look and act like a traditional robot, which would sit inside the car and drive the vehicle, but this is not likely in the near-term and certainly not prior to the advent of today's version of self-driving cars).

I've exhorted that we are going to find ourselves confronted with a "head nod" problem, whereby as pedestrians we can no longer look at the head of the driver to get subtle but telling clues about what the driver is intending to do.

Thus, this vital social interaction is going to be broken, meaning that the pedestrian won't know what the AI driving system is "thinking" (there's not as yet a theory-of-mind that we can have about AI driving systems), and likewise, the AI if not properly developed won't be gauging what the pedestrian might do.

There are various technological solutions being explored to deal with this social interaction, including for example putting LED displays on the exterior of the car to provide info to pedestrians, and there is the hope that V2P (vehicle-to-pedestrian) electronic messaging will help, though all of this has yet to be figured out.

Let's tie this together with the earlier equations presented.

A self-driving car is coming down the street and meanwhile, a pedestrian is getting ready to jaywalk.

We are on the verge of a social interaction, namely a 1R <-> 1H situation.

The AI of the self-driving car wants to stand its ground and intends to proceed unabated, so it somehow communicates this to the pedestrian, attempting a 1R -> 1H.

In what way will the communication occur, and will the human pedestrian acquiesce or resist and opt to jaywalk?

That's yet to be well-formulated.

Let's bump things up.

A group of strangers are standing on a street corner, waiting to cross the street (this is nH).

As a self-driving car reaches the corner, it wants to try and make sure that those pedestrians stand away from the corner, since the AI system is going to make that right turn without pausing.

We have this: 1R -> nH

It could be that the pedestrians do nothing and standstill.

Or, they might look at each other and try to figure out which has the greater will, namely they as a pack of humans might decide to flow off the curb into the street, doing so to basically tell the self-driving car to back off and let them cross, though it could also be that they briefly confer and decide that it is better to let the AI do its things and make the turn.

In essence, this happened: 1R -> nH: nH <-> nH.

A key point here is that the AI system is acting as a social actor that is communicating in some fashion, whether well-articulated or poorly devised, and conveying to a group of humans what it (the AI) is aiming to do, and among the humans this potentially sparks a group interaction, leading then to a myriad of potential outcomes.

And, by the way, the outcomes involved can readily be of a life-or-death nature.

That's why this particular kind of AI system, a self-driving car, deserves some really close and thoughtful consideration about what it is and how it will work and what it will do.

Including especially how it interacts with humans and how it impacts social interaction among humans.

One could argue that unlike perhaps a lot of other AI systems, there are much higher risks surrounding AI driving systems.

Fortunately, there are increasing wake-up calls about the role of social interaction in the emergence of AI self-driving cars.

One of the co-authors of the Yale study is Professor Nicholas Christakis, who has expressed in a piece in *The Atlantic* this important point: "Driving is a very modern kind of social interaction, requiring high levels of cooperation and social coordination."

That's a vital point.

Sadly, regrettably, ominously, many of the automakers and self-driving tech makers sometimes have given short shrift to the social interaction facets of self-driving cars (instead, those builders are often focused on the engineering and tech, alone, and eschew consideration for the social interaction elements of driving).

I'll give the last word to Dr. Christakis as he hits the nail-on-the-head upon bringing up the importance of social spillovers of AI, making this crucial insight: "… we would be reckless to unleash new forms of AI without first taking such social spillovers, or externalities, as they're often called, into account."

It's a cruel world out there.

In the case of AI systems for self-driving cars, we know that today's human drivers socially interact with other human drivers and with pedestrians, doing so in an often harsh and demanding dog-eat-dog dance, occurring each day on our highways, byways, and neighborhood streets, over the course of some 2.5 trillion miles driven.

We need to make sure that the AI self-driving car is a social actor equally up to the same task.

CHAPTER 11
MEDICAL EMERGENCIES AND AI SELF-DRIVING CARS

CHAPTER 11

MEDICAL EMERGENCIES

AND

AI SELF-DRIVING CARS

Jonathan got into his car that morning and was driving over to the grocery store. It was a day like any other day. He had driven the route many times before.

Suddenly, while at the wheel, he began to suffer a heart attack.

Grabbing his chest, he lost consciousness and blacked out.

Unfortunately, he also lost utter control of the car and the vehicle barreled into another nearby car, harming its occupants, and then careened onto the sidewalk, injuring pedestrians walking innocently along.

According to stats published by in the National Motor Vehicle Crash Causation Survey (NMVCCS), here is the frequency of medical emergencies impacting a human driver during their time at the wheel and involving a car crash:

- Seizure: 35%
- Sudden blackout: 29%
- Diabetic Reaction: 20%
- Heart Attack: 11%
- Stroke: 3%
- Other: 4%

These are rounded numbers, and they also are indicative of the primary medical ailment, which notably a person can incur more than one such adverse malady in each such car crash.

Most people probably don't realize that a car driver can be relieved of all liability for a car crash if they perchance suffer a sudden medical emergency while driving a car (it's a well-known defense tactic among automotive attorneys).

This might seem like a shocking notion, namely that a driver can be absolved of their driving responsibilities simply due to incurring a personal medical urgency. There is though a set of criteria that must be met, including that the driver was unable to anticipate or foresee that they might suffer the medical issue and that the matter directly caused the driver to lose control of the car.

With the advent of true self-driving cars, there won't be a human driver at the wheel, therefore we'll no longer need to worry about human drivers that lose control of driving due to medical emergencies while inside a driverless car.

There though is still a problem afoot.

If you are a passenger in a self-driving car and suffer a medical emergency, there isn't a human driver available to immediately tend to you, which there would be if you were in today's ridesharing vehicles (where a human driver is needed).

Furthermore, even if a ridesharing driver or other driver was not able to attend to you, they would at least recognize that you are suffering a medical emergency and presumably try to take some constructive action, perhaps hitting the gas pedal and speeding over to the nearest hospital.

Here's then an interesting and important question: *What will happen if a passenger in a self-driving car suffers a medical emergency and how will the AI system that is driving the car respond?*

In case you think this is a so-called edge problem, a phrase used by many in the driverless car industry to refer to rare use cases that are unlikely to ever occur, I wouldn't be so fast to assume that medical emergencies of passengers in self-driving cars are going to be quite so infrequent.

You can bet that there are going to be a number of instances involving someone having a medical emergency while riding in a driverless car, especially since the prediction is that we are heading toward a mobility-for-all era due to the advent of self-driving cars.

More people will be riding in cars, more of the time, and including people today that are mobility marginalized or mobility disadvantaged.

The medical question about handling humans that have encountered a problem is going to become readily apparent once there are thousands or eventually millions of driverless cars roaming around and giving us rides.

Let's unpack the matter.

The Levels Of Self-Driving Cars

It is important to clarify what I mean when referring to true self-driving cars.

True self-driving cars are ones that the AI drives the car entirely on its own and there isn't any human assistance during the driving task.

These driverless cars are considered a Level 4 and Level 5, while a car that requires a human driver to co-share the driving effort is usually considered at a Level 2 or Level 3. The cars that co-share the driving task are described as being semi-autonomous, and typically contain a variety of automated add-ons that are referred to as ADAS (Advanced Driver-Assistance Systems).

There is not yet a true self-driving car at Level 5, which we don't yet even know if this will be possible to achieve, and nor how long it will take to get there.

Meanwhile, the Level 4 efforts are gradually trying to get some traction by undergoing very narrow and selective public roadway trials, though there is controversy over whether this testing should be allowed per se (we are all life-or-death guinea pigs in an experiment taking place on our highways and byways, some point out).

Since the semi-autonomous cars require a human driver, such cars will only somewhat moderately alter today's practices of what happens when there is a medical emergency inside a car.

First, if the medical emergency is suffered by a passenger, the driver is in essentially the same boat as they are today. It would be up to the driver to decide what to do next, whether to pull over and assist the passenger or to speed to a hospital.

One unfortunate consequence of having the ADAS features will be that the driver might be tempted to take their attention away from the driving task and attempt to attend to the passenger.

This is somewhat akin to today's drivers that you see in online videos while driving a Level 2 or Level 3 car and are showcasing themselves asleep at the wheel or playing a game on their smartphone. Those dolts don't seem to realize that they are the responsible party for the driving actions of the car, regardless of how much automation might be tossed into a Level 2 or Level 3.

We can all be sympathetic that if a driver is driving a Level 2 or Level 3 car and a dear friend that's riding along begins to suffer a heart attack, there is a tremendous temptation to turn away from the wheel of the car to help out their stricken pal. The driver assumes that the ADAS can keep things going while they, the human, divert their attention.

Regrettably, this is a tall risk for everyone else.

Any cars nearby or any pedestrians, bicyclists, motorcyclists, or others that can get hit are now at heightened risk the moment the driver is no longer focusing on the driving task.

One wonders whether this will open a new can of worms, allowing attorneys to come up with a variant of the sudden medical emergency defense, though in this case, the driver is not suffering the medical emergency and instead giving up momentarily their responsibility overseeing the car to try and care for someone else within the car.

With today's conventional cars, I doubt that any reasonable party would go along with the notion that a driver diverted their attention to aid someone else in the car since we all know that a conventional car can become an unguided missile. The aspect that a Level 2 or Level 3 can kind of drive the car for you, opens the idea that maybe we can sometimes make a judgment call about the risk of a car striking someone else versus the desire to aid an ailing passenger.

This also brings us to the other salient aspect about a Level 2 and Level 3 car and involves the use case of the driver themselves suffering a medical emergency.

For some of the semi-autonomous cars, the automakers are including sensors to detect whether the driver is attending to the driving task. For example, a sensor on the steering wheel might detect the presence of your hands. Or, a camera might be facing inward and pointed at your head, scanning the position of your face and eyes, doing so to ascertain whether you are looking straight ahead at the road.

If those devices determine that you don't seem to be watching the road, they will usually generate an audio alert such a buzzing sound to let the driver know that something is amiss. It could be that the driver has dozed off, or maybe the driver is drunk and not properly focusing on the driving task.

If the driver does not respond to the alert, the ADAS features are typically being programmed to gradually decrease the speed of the car and come to an eventual halt. The stopping action might occur within the lane that the car is already positioned in, or if the ADAS is more advanced it will try to pull to the side of the road.

As might be apparent, the feature of detecting the driver's attention could certainly help in cases of a driver that suffers a sudden medical emergency. Plus, you could suggest that the driver that attends to an ailing passenger would also be able to rely upon the ADAS to gradually stop the car while the driver tries to provide medical aid.

The rub is that we don't yet know how this will all play out in the real world.

Keep in mind that we'll have a mixture of levels of cars for many years to come.

For those driving conventional cars, will they realize that a car ahead of them that is slowing down is something to be carefully avoided, presumably being a Level 2 or Level 3 that has taken over (somewhat, weakly) the full control of the driving of the car?

Also, if an ADAS equipped car slows down and stops in the middle of traffic, though this seems like a suitable solution, keep in mind that a conventional car might approach this stopped car and unknowingly ram into it. The stopped car might be on a stretch of road that's around a bend, or maybe it is nighttime and very dark, therefore other drivers aren't expecting to find cars that are just plunked down in the middle of the lanes and at a dead stop.

The overall point is that the Level 2 and Level 3 are not going to be a savior for those instances of drivers that suffer medical emergencies, and nor necessarily be the best solution when a driver wants to attend to a passenger.

We really don't yet know how other drivers will react and whether these seemingly safety approaches of crudely and gradually bringing an amiss car to a stop is going to work out well or not.

True Self-Driving Cars Aspects

Next, let's examine how medical emergencies would be handled by a Level 4 or Level 5 driverless car.

We can put aside the case of a human driver that becomes unable to drive an autonomous car since there won't be a human driver. This though does not mean that there won't be human drivers of cars less than a Level 4, of which those drivers might still suffer medical emergencies and then ram into a true self-driving car.

Consider what needs to happen when a passenger in a driverless car is suffering a medical emergency.

I think we'd all hope that the AI would be programmed sufficiently to try and recognize that a passenger is suffering a medical ailment.

Of course, this might not be on the list of priorities for the automakers and tech firms that are currently crafting driverless cars. For right now, the topmost importance is being able to have the AI drive the car, doing so safely and reliably. Dealing with passenger mishaps is not at the height of their requirements list.

You could shift the detection aspects over to the human passenger, suggesting that it is up to the passenger to let the AI know that something is amiss.

Maybe the passenger yells out a codeword that's been prearranged. Perhaps the passenger screams and the audio picks up the screaming. Think of this like an Alexa or Siri kind of capability.

Part of the problem with these methods of alerting the AI is that the AI won't "know" whether the passenger is in trouble versus just playing around. Maybe you are partying inside the driverless car and so the sound of screaming is due to the fun being had.

Automakers are tending toward using an OnStar-like service to help deal with these situations. Rather than the AI having to figure out what's going on, the assumption is that the passenger will invoke the OnStar-like capability and get connected to a remote human. The remote human will then interact with the passenger and try to ascertain what's happening.

The remote human might be able to take over the driving of the self-driving car, though I've warned about the dangers of allowing this to happen, or they might instead offer directives to the self-driving car about what to do (such as telling the driverless car to pull over or drive to the nearest hospital, for which the AI then does the driving and not the remote human).

At a future point, presumably, the AI will be sharp enough that a human remote agent is not needed.

This would reduce the size of the labor force that would otherwise need to be assembled to handle the widespread advent of self-driving cars (think about how large a staff you'd need if there were millions of driverless cars on the roadways and remote humans were needed to assist).

Plus, there is always the chance that the remote communication feature is blocked or unable to be used due to an electronic communications issue. It would behoove everyone if the AI that's already "on-board" the car could deal with these situations.

One assumes that a sophisticated AI system might be able to use facial recognition to ascertain whether a passenger is potentially in pain. By using an inward-facing camera, the AI might be able to detect not only facial expressions, but also notice that a person has slumped over, or maybe their speech is slurred, and so on.

The same telltale clues that we use to assess whether someone is medically distressed could be used by an AI system.

Let's then assume that one way or another the aspect that a passenger is suffering a medical emergency is determinable and that the AI is thusly notified that an occurrence is underway.

What then?

With a human driver, the driver might panic and make matters worse.

In theory, the AI shouldn't panic and shouldn't make the matter worse.

As they say, first do no harm.

The AI cannot physically attend to the ailing passenger, which a human driver could have done. Therefore, presumably, the AI cannot lend a helping hand, as it were.

This could be somewhat ameliorated if there were medical devices inside the driverless car. The possibility exists that someone could outfit the driverless car with various medical equipment, anticipating that someday a medical emergency might require the devices.

The AI could urge the passenger to put on or otherwise get coupled with the onboard medical devices, and then perhaps the AI itself would direct those medical devices to operate.

I'm sure that any medical doctor or nurse is right now shuddering to think that such a thing might be put in place.

Do we want an AI system to be acting as though it is rendering medical aid?

Well, like it or not, we are seemingly headed in that direction anyway. More and more, we'll see healthcare being undertaken by AI systems that aid us humans during medical moments. That's a tide that is coming toward us all.

Conclusion

Besides offering a bedside manner to a passenger, the AI should also ascertain what to do about the car and where the car is headed.

This might be discussed with the passenger and the AI's Natural Language Processing (NLP) component could attempt to work out a plan of action with the suffering rider.

The passenger might be totally incapacitated, or unconscious, or might still be conscious but not in full use of their faculties. In which case, the AI will need to decide what to do.

The good news is that during the medical emergency, the AI is still driving the car, doing so as safely and properly as if there wasn't a medical urgency taking place. That's the no panic part of the AI driving equation.

Suppose the AI determines that routing the car to the nearest hospital or emergency room is the prudent course of action. It would be a relatively simple matter for the AI to reroute the driverless car accordingly.

There are some added pluses possible too.

The AI might use its V2V (vehicle-to-vehicle) electronic communications to ask other nearby cars to get out of the way and open a faster path for getting to the medical services. Likewise, the use of V2I (vehicle-to-infrastructure) electronic communications could tell the traffic signals to go to green and allow the driverless car to zip along, akin to what some ambulances and firetrucks can do today with traffic lights.

Would we be willing to have self-driving cars drive over the speed limit in such cases?

I ask the question because there are some that insist that driverless cars should never break the law and will always drive in strictly legal ways. I've debunked this idea and pointed out that we'll need to consider situations whereby "illegal" driving might be permitted.

There are additional interesting twists involved.

For example, suppose another driverless car is taking a medical doctor to the opera (of course, it has to be an opera).

The self-driving car with the passenger in a medical emergency could use V2V to inform the other driverless car that a rider needs urgent medical care. The medical doctor, getting notified via the AI of his driverless car, agrees to help.

The two driverless cars now calculate the fastest route to meet up. Upon the rendezvous, the doctor gets into the self-driving car with the ailing passenger and begins to render medical assistance. At this point, the self-driving car might then rush to the hospital.

What has been gained by the rendezvous?

It could be that the medical doctor was in a driverless car that was just one minute away, while the nearest hospital is twenty minutes away. Nearly immediate medical care could be arranged in such a scenario. Similarly, an ambulance or firetruck could have been contacted to make a mid-journey rendezvous.

Medical care on the go and other facets of dealing with medical emergencies will be reshaped as the emergence of self-driving cars takes place.

Maybe we need to get the AI to take the Hippocratic oath.

APPENDIX

APPENDIX A
TEACHING WITH THIS MATERIAL

The material in this book can be readily used either as a supplemental to other content for a class, or it can also be used as a core set of textbook material for a specialized class. Classes where this material is most likely used include any classes at the college or university level that want to augment the class by offering thought provoking and educational essays about AI and self-driving cars.

In particular, here are some aspects for class use:

o   Computer Science. Studying AI, autonomous vehicles, etc.

o   Business. Exploring technology and it adoption for business.

o   Sociology. Sociological views on the adoption and advancement of technology.

Specialized classes at the undergraduate and graduate level can also make use of this material.

For each chapter, consider whether you think the chapter provides material relevant to your course topic. There is plenty of opportunity to get the students thinking about the topic and force them to decide whether they agree or disagree with the points offered and positions taken. I would also encourage you to have the students do additional research beyond the chapter material presented (I provide next some suggested assignments they can do).

RESEARCH ASSIGNMENTS ON THESE TOPICS

Your students can find background material on these topics, doing so in various business and technical publications. I list below the top ranked AI related journals. For business publications, I would suggest the usual culprits such as the Harvard Business Review, Forbes, Fortune, WSJ, and the like.

Here are some suggestions of homework or projects that you could assign to students:

a) Assignment for foundational AI research topic: Research and prepare a paper and a presentation on a specific aspect of Deep AI, Machine Learning, ANN, etc. The paper should cite at least 3 reputable sources. Compare and contrast to what has been stated in this book.

b) Assignment for the Self-Driving Car topic: Research and prepare a paper and Self-Driving Cars. Cite at least 3 reputable sources and analyze the characterizations. Compare and contrast to what has been stated in this book.

c) Assignment for a Business topic: Research and prepare a paper and a presentation on businesses and advanced technology. What is hot, and what is not? Cite at least 3 reputable sources. Compare and contrast to the depictions in this book.

d) Assignment to do a Startup: Have the students prepare a paper about how they might startup a business in this realm. They must submit a sound Business Plan for the startup. They could also be asked to present their Business Plan and so should also have a presentation deck to coincide with it.

You can certainly adjust the aforementioned assignments to fit to your particular needs and the class structure. You'll notice that I ask for 3 reputable cited sources for the paper writing based assignments. I usually steer students toward "reputable" publications, since otherwise they will cite some oddball source that has no credentials other than that they happened to write something and post it onto the Internet. You can define "reputable" in whatever way you prefer, for example some faculty think Wikipedia is not reputable while others believe it is reputable and allow students to cite it.

The reason that I usually ask for at least 3 citations is that if the student only does one or two citations they usually settle on whatever they happened to find the fastest. By requiring three citations, it usually seems to force them to look around, explore, and end-up probably finding five or more, and then whittling it down to 3 that they will actually use.

I have not specified the length of their papers, and leave that to you to tell the students what you prefer. For each of those assignments, you could end-up with a short one to two pager, or you could do a dissertation length paper. Base the length on whatever best fits for your class, and the credit amount of the assignment within the context of the other grading metrics you'll be using for the class.

I mention in the assignments that they are to do a paper and prepare a presentation. I usually try to get students to present their work. This is a good practice for what they will do in the business world. Most of the time, they will be required to prepare an analysis and present it. If you don't have the class time or inclination to have the students present, then you can of course cut out the aspect of them putting together a presentation.

If you want to point students toward highly ranked journals in AI, here's a list of the top journals as reported by *various citation counts sources* (this list changes year to year):

- Communications of the ACM
- Artificial Intelligence
- Cognitive Science
- IEEE Transactions on Pattern Analysis and Machine Intelligence
- Foundations and Trends in Machine Learning
- Journal of Memory and Language
- Cognitive Psychology
- Neural Networks
- IEEE Transactions on Neural Networks and Learning Systems
- IEEE Intelligent Systems
- Knowledge-based Systems

GUIDE TO USING THE CHAPTERS

For each of the chapters, I provide next some various ways to use the chapter material. You can assign the tasks as individual homework assignments, or the tasks can be used with team projects for the class. You can easily layout a series of assignments, such as indicating that the students are to do item "a" below for say Chapter 1, then "b" for the next chapter of the book, and so on.

a) What is the main point of the chapter and describe in your own words the significance of the topic,

b) Identify at least two aspects in the chapter that you agree with, and support your concurrence by providing at least one other outside researched item as support; make sure to explain your basis for disagreeing with the aspects,

c) Identify at least two aspects in the chapter that you disagree with, and support your disagreement by providing at least one other outside researched item as support; make sure to explain your basis for disagreeing with the aspects,

d) Find an aspect that was not covered in the chapter, doing so by conducting outside research, and then explain how that aspect ties into the chapter and what significance it brings to the topic,

e) Interview a specialist in industry about the topic of the chapter, collect from them their thoughts and opinions, and readdress the chapter by citing your source and how they compared and contrasted to the material,

f) Interview a relevant academic professor or researcher in a college or university about the topic of the chapter, collect from them their thoughts and opinions, and readdress the chapter by citing your source and how they compared and contrasted to the material,

g) Try to update a chapter by finding out the latest on the topic, and ascertain whether the issue or topic has now been solved or whether it is still being addressed, explain what you come up with.

The above are all ways in which you can get the students of your class involved in considering the material of a given chapter. You could mix things up by having one of those above assignments per each week, covering the chapters over the course of the semester or quarter.

As a reminder, here are the chapters of the book and you can select whichever chapters you find most valued for your particular class:

Chapter Title

1 Eliot Framework for AI Self-Driving Cars

2 Non-Driving Robots and AI Self-Driving Cars

3 HealthTech and AI Self-Driving Cars

4 Rudest Drivers and AI Self-Driving Cars

5 Aliens On Earth and AI Self-Driving Cars

6 AI Human Rights and AI Self-Driving Cars

7 Pope's AI Ethics and AI Self-Driving Cars

8 Human Judgment and AI Self-Driving Cars

9 DoD AI Ethics and AI Self-Driving Cars

10 Group Dynamics and AI Self-Driving Cars

11 Medical Emergencies Inside AI Self-Driving Cars

Companion Book By This Author

Advances in AI and Autonomous Vehicles: Cybernetic Self-Driving Cars

Practical Advances in Artificial Intelligence (AI) and Machine Learning

by

Dr. Lance B. Eliot, MBA, PhD

This title is available via Amazon and other book sellers

Companion Book By This Author

Self-Driving Cars:
"The Mother of All AI Projects"

by Dr. Lance B. Eliot, MBA, PhD

This title is available via Amazon and other book sellers

Companion Book By This Author

Innovation and Thought Leadership on Self-Driving Driverless Cars

by Dr. Lance B. Eliot, MBA, PhD

This title is available via Amazon and other book sellers

Companion Book By This Author

New Advances in AI Autonomous Driverless Cars Self-Driving Cars

by Dr. Lance B. Eliot, MBA, PhD

This title is available via Amazon and other book sellers

Companion Book By This Author

Companion Book By This Author

Introduction to
Driverless Self-Driving Cars

by Dr. Lance B. Eliot, MBA, PhD

Chapter Title

This title is available via Amazon and other book sellers

Companion Book By This Author

Autonomous Vehicle Driverless
Self-Driving Cars and Artificial Intelligence

by Dr. Lance B. Eliot, MBA, PhD

This title is available via Amazon and other book sellers

<u>Companion Book By This Author</u>

Transformative Artificial Intelligence Driverless Self-Driving Cars

by Dr. Lance B. Eliot, MBA, PhD

<u>Chapter Title</u>

This title is available via Amazon and other book sellers

Companion Book By This Author

Disruptive Artificial Intelligence
and Driverless Self-Driving Cars

by Dr. Lance B. Eliot, MBA, PhD

This title is available via Amazon and other book sellers

Companion Book By This Author

State-of-the-Art
AI Driverless Self-Driving Cars

by Dr. Lance B. Eliot, MBA, PhD

This title is available via Amazon and other book sellers

Companion Book By This Author

Top Trends in
AI Self-Driving Cars

by Dr. Lance B. Eliot, MBA, PhD

This title is available via Amazon and other book sellers

Companion Book By This Author

AI Innovations and Self-Driving Cars

by Dr. Lance B. Eliot, MBA, PhD

Chapter Title

1 Eliot Framework for AI Self-Driving Cars

2 API's and Self-Driving Cars

3 Egocentric Designs and Self-Driving Cars

4 Family Road Trip and Self-Driving Cars

5 AI Developer Burnout and Tesla Car Crash

6 Stealing Secrets About Self-Driving Cars

7 Affordability and Self-Driving Cars

8 Crossing the Rubicon and Self-Driving Cars

9 Addicted to Self-Driving Cars

10 Ultrasonic Harm and Self-Driving Cars

11 Accidents Contagion and Self-Driving Cars

12 Non-Stop 24x7 and Self-Driving Cars

13 Human Life Spans and Self-Driving Cars

This title is available via Amazon and other book sellers

Companion Book By This Author

Crucial Advances for
AI Self-Driving Cars

by Dr. Lance B. Eliot, MBA, PhD

Chapter Title

This title is available via Amazon and other book sellers

Companion Book By This Author

Sociotechnical Insights and
AI Driverless Cars

by Dr. Lance B. Eliot, MBA, PhD

Chapter Title

This title is available via Amazon and other book sellers

<u>Companion Book By This Author</u>

Pioneering Advances for AI Driverless Cars

by Dr. Lance B. Eliot, MBA, PhD

<u>Chapter Title</u>

This title is available via Amazon and other book sellers

Companion Book By This Author

Leading Edge Trends for
AI Driverless Cars

by Dr. Lance B. Eliot, MBA, PhD

This title is available via Amazon and other book sellers

This title is available via Amazon and other book sellers

Companion Book By This Author

The Next Wave of
AI Self-Driving Cars

by Dr. Lance B. Eliot, MBA, PhD

This title is available via Amazon and other book sellers

Revolutionary Innovations of
AI Self-Driving Cars

by Dr. Lance B. Eliot, MBA, PhD

Chapter Title

This title is available via Amazon and other book sellers

Companion Book By This Author

AI Self-Driving Cars
Breakthroughs

by Dr. Lance B. Eliot, MBA, PhD

Chapter Title

This title is available via Amazon and other book sellers

Trailblazing Trends for
AI Self-Driving Cars

by Dr. Lance B. Eliot, MBA, PhD

Companion Book By This Author

Ingenious Strides for
AI Driverless Cars

by Dr. Lance B. Eliot, MBA, PhD

Chapter Title

This title is available via Amazon and other book sellers

Companion Book By This Author

AI Self-Driving Cars
Inventiveness

by Dr. Lance B. Eliot, MBA, PhD

This title is available via Amazon and other book sellers

Companion Book By This Author

Visionary Secrets of
AI Driverless Cars

by Dr. Lance B. Eliot, MBA, PhD

This title is available via Amazon and other book sellers

Companion Book By This Author

Spearheading
AI Self-Driving Cars

by Dr. Lance B. Eliot, MBA, PhD

Chapter Title

This title is available via Amazon and other book sellers

Companion Book By This Author

Spurring
AI Self-Driving Cars
by Dr. Lance B. Eliot, MBA, PhD

This title is available via Amazon and other book sellers

Companion Book By This Author

Avant-Garde
AI Driverless Cars

by Dr. Lance B. Eliot, MBA, PhD

This title is available via Amazon and other book sellers

Companion Book By This Author

AI Self-Driving Cars
Evolvement

by Dr. Lance B. Eliot, MBA, PhD

Chapter Title

This title is available via Amazon and other book sellers

Companion Book By This Author

AI Driverless Cars
Chrysalis
by Dr. Lance B. Eliot, MBA, PhD

This title is available via Amazon and other book sellers

Companion Book By This Author

Boosting
AI Autonomous Cars
by Dr. Lance B. Eliot, MBA, PhD

This title is available via Amazon and other book sellers

Companion Book By This Author

AI Self-Driving Cars Trendsetting

by Dr. Lance B. Eliot, MBA, PhD

This title is available via Amazon and other book sellers

Dr. Lance B. Eliot

<u>Companion Book By This Author</u>

AI Autonomous Cars
Forefront

by Dr. Lance B. Eliot, MBA, PhD

<u>Chapter Title</u>

This title is available via Amazon and other book sellers

Companion Book By This Author

AI Autonomous Cars Emergence

by Dr. Lance B. Eliot, MBA, PhD

This title is available via Amazon and other book sellers

Companion Book By This Author

AI Autonomous Cars Progress

by Dr. Lance B. Eliot, MBA, PhD

Chapter Title

This title is available via Amazon and other book sellers

Companion Book By This Author

AI Self-Driving Cars Prognosis

by Dr. Lance B. Eliot, MBA, PhD

This title is available via Amazon and other book sellers

Companion Book By This Author

AI Self-Driving Cars
Momentum

by Dr. Lance B. Eliot, MBA, PhD

This title is available via Amazon and other book sellers

Companion Book By This Author

AI Self-Driving Cars
Headway

by Dr. Lance B. Eliot, MBA, PhD

<u>Chapter Title</u>

1   Eliot Framework for AI Self-Driving Cars

2   Germs Spreading and AI Self-Driving Cars

3   Carbon Footprint and AI Self-Driving Cars

4   Protestors Use Of AI Self-Driving Cars

5   Rogue Behavior and AI Self-Driving Cars

6   Using Human Drivers Versus AI Self-Driving Cars

7   Tesla Hodge-Podge On AI Self-Driving Cars

8   Solo Occupancy and AI Self-Driving Cars

9   Einstein's Twins Paradox and AI Self-Driving Cars

10   Nation-State Takeover Of AI Self-Driving Cars

11   Quantum Computers and AI Self-Driving Cars

12   Religious Revival And AI Self-Driving Cars

This title is available via Amazon and other book sellers

Dr. Lance B. Eliot

Companion Book By This Author

AI Self-Driving Cars
Vicissitude

by Dr. Lance B. Eliot, MBA, PhD

Chapter Title

This title is available via Amazon and other book sellers

Companion Book By This Author

AI Self-Driving Cars
Autonomy
by Dr. Lance B. Eliot, MBA, PhD

This title is available via Amazon and other book sellers

Companion Book By This Author

AI Driverless Cars Transmutation

by Dr. Lance B. Eliot, MBA, PhD

This title is available via Amazon and other book sellers

Dr. Lance B. Eliot

<u>Companion Book By This Author</u>

AI Driverless Cars
Potentiality

by Dr. Lance B. Eliot, MBA, PhD

<u>Chapter Title</u>

1 Eliot Framework for AI Self-Driving Cars

2 Russian Values and AI Self-Driving Cars

3 Friendships Uplift and AI Self-Driving Cars

4 Dogs Driving and AI Self-Driving Cars

5 Hypodermic Needles and AI Self-Driving Cars

6 Sharing Self-Driving Tech Is Not Likely

7 Uber Driver "Kidnapper" Is Self-Driving Car Lesson

8 Gender Driving Biases In AI Self-Driving Cars

9 Slain Befriended Dolphins Are Self-Driving Car Lesson

10 Analysis Of AI In Government Report

11 Mobility Frenzy and AI Self-Driving Cars

This title is available via Amazon and other book sellers

<u>Companion Book By This Author</u>

AI Driverless Cars
Realities

by Dr. Lance B. Eliot, MBA, PhD

This title is available via Amazon and other book sellers

ABOUT THE AUTHOR

Dr. Lance B. Eliot, MBA, PhD is the CEO of Techbruim, Inc. and Executive Director of the Cybernetic AI Self-Driving Car Institute and has over twenty years of industry experience including serving as a corporate officer in a billion dollar firm and was a partner in a major executive services firm. He is also a serial entrepreneur having founded, ran, and sold several high-tech related businesses. He previously hosted the popular radio show *Technotrends* that was also available on American Airlines flights via their in-flight audio program. Author or co-author of a dozen books and over 400 articles, he has made appearances on CNN, and has been a frequent speaker at industry conferences.

A former professor at the University of Southern California (USC), he founded and led an innovative research lab on Artificial Intelligence in Business. Known as the "AI Insider" his writings on AI advances and trends has been widely read and cited. He also previously served on the faculty of the University of California Los Angeles (UCLA), and was a visiting professor at other major universities. He was elected to the International Board of the Society for Information Management (SIM), a prestigious association of over 3,000 high-tech executives worldwide.

He has performed extensive community service, including serving as Senior Science Adviser to the Vice Chair of the Congressional Committee on Science & Technology. He has served on the Board of the OC Science & Engineering Fair (OCSEF), where he is also has been a Grand Sweepstakes judge, and likewise served as a judge for the Intel International SEF (ISEF). He served as the Vice Chair of the Association for Computing Machinery (ACM) Chapter, a prestigious association of computer scientists. Dr. Eliot has been a shark tank judge for the USC Mark Stevens Center for Innovation on start-up pitch competitions, and served as a mentor for several incubators and accelerators in Silicon Valley and Silicon Beach. He served on several Boards and Committees at USC, including having served on the Marshall Alumni Association (MAA) Board in Southern California.

Dr. Eliot holds a PhD from USC, MBA, and Bachelor's in Computer Science, and earned the CDP, CCP, CSP, CDE, and CISA certifications. Born and raised in Southern California, and having traveled and lived internationally, he enjoys scuba diving, surfing, and sailing.

ADDENDUM

AI Driverless Cars Realities

*Practical Advances in Artificial Intelligence (AI)
and Machine Learning*

By

Dr. Lance B. Eliot, MBA, PhD

———

For supplemental materials of this book, visit:

www.ai-selfdriving-cars.guru

For special orders of this book, contact:

LBE Press Publishing

Email: LBE.Press.Publishing@gmail.com